WeightWatchers®

Stir It Up!
Super
Skillet Cookbook

A Word About Weight Watchers

Since 1963, Weight Watchers has grown from a handful of people to millions of enrollments annually. Today, Weight Watchers is recognized as the leading name in safe and sensible weight control. Weight Watchers members form diverse groups, from youths to senior citizens, attending meetings virtually around the globe. Weight-loss and weight-management results vary by individual, but we recommend that you attend Weight Watchers meetings to benefit from the supportive environment you'll find there and follow the comprehensive Weight Watchers program which includes food plans, an activity plan, and a thinking skills plan. For the Weight Watchers meeting nearest you, call **800-651-6000**. Also, visit us at our Web site, **www.WeightWatchers.com**, or look for *Weight Watchers* Magazine at your newsstand or in your meeting room.

 **CORE PLAN** RECIPE   20 MINUTES OR LESS   VEGETARIAN

Shiitake-Chicken Stir-Fry, page 66

WEIGHT WATCHERS PUBLISHING GROUP

CREATIVE AND EDITORIAL DIRECTOR	**NANCY GAGLIARDI**
ART DIRECTOR	**ED MELNITSKY**
PRODUCTION MANAGER	**ALAN BIEDERMAN**
ASSOCIATE ART DIRECTOR	**JENNIFER BOWLES**
OFFICE MANAGER AND PUBLISHING ASSISTANT	**JENNY LABOY-BRACE**
FOOD EDITOR	**CAROL PRAGER**
FOOD CONSULTANT	**EILEEN RUNYAN**
NUTRITION CONSULTANT	**PATTY SANTELLI**
PHOTOGRAPHER	**RITA MAAS**
FOOD STYLIST	**MICHAEL PEDERSON**
PROP STYLIST	**BETTE BLAU**
DESIGN/PRODUCTION	**LYNDA D'AMICO**

ON THE COVER: Southwestern Skillet Macaroni and Cheese, page 92 (with a *POINTS*® value of only 6)

About Our Recipes

We make every effort to ensure that you will have success with our recipes. For best results and for nutritional accuracy, please keep the following guidelines in mind:

● Recipes in this book have been developed for Weight Watchers members who are following either the **Core Plan** or the **Flex Plan** on the **TurnAround**™ program. All **Core Plan** recipes are marked with our **Core Plan** recipe icon ☑. We include *POINTS*® values so you can use any of the recipes if you are following the **Flex Plan** on the program. *POINTS* values are assigned based on calories, fat (grams), and fiber (grams) provided for a serving size of a recipe.

● All recipes feature approximate nutritional information; our recipes are analyzed for Calories (Cal), Total Fat (Fat), Saturated Fat (Sat Fat), Trans Fat (Trans Fat), Cholesterol (Chol), Sodium (Sod), Carbohydrates (Carb), Dietary Fiber (Fib), Protein (Prot), and Calcium (Calc).

● Nutritional information for recipes that include meat, poultry, and fish are based on cooked skinless boneless portions (unless otherwise stated), with the fat trimmed.

● We recommend that you buy lean meat and poultry, then trim it of all visible fat before cooking. When poultry is cooked with the skin on, we suggest removing the skin before eating.

● Before serving, divide foods—including any vegetables, sauce, or accompaniments—into portions of equal size according to the designated number of servings per recipe.

● Any substitutions made to the ingredients will alter the "Per serving" nutritional information and may affect the **Core Plan** recipe status or the *POINTS* value.

● It is implied that all fresh fruits, vegetables, and greens in recipes should be rinsed before using.

Sesame-Crusted Swordfish
with Scallion Sauce, page 148

Contents

Stir-Fry Classics

CHAPTER 1

Ginger Beef and Asparagus Stir-Fry

PREP 20 MINUTES PLUS 1 HOUR MARINATING TIME
COOK ABOUT 10 MINUTES
SERVES 4

1 Combine the wine, soy sauce, ginger, and garlic in a zip-close plastic bag; add the steak. Squeeze out the air and seal the bag; turn to coat the steak. Refrigerate, turning the bag occasionally, at least 1 hour. Drain the steak, reserving the marinade.

2 Heat a large nonstick skillet or wok over high heat until a drop of water sizzles. Add 1 teaspoon of the oil, swirl to coat the pan, then add the steak. Stir-fry until cooked through, 3–4 minutes. Transfer the steak to a plate and set aside.

3 Add the remaining 1 teaspoon oil to the skillet, swirl to coat the pan, then add the leek. Stir-fry until softened, 4–5 minutes. Add the chili paste (if using) and stir-fry until fragrant, about 5 seconds. Stir in the steak, the reserved marinade, the asparagus, carrot, and the dissolved cornstarch; cook, stirring gently, until the sauce thickens, about 2 minutes.

PER SERVING (1 ½ cups): 154 Cal, 5 g Fat, 1 g Sat Fat, 1 g Trans Fat, 33 mg Chol, 198 mg Sod, 10 g Carb, 2 g Fib, 15 g Prot, 41 mg Calc. *POINTS* value: *3.*

HOW WE DID IT To steam the asparagus and carrot before stir-frying, place the asparagus in a steamer basket set in a saucepan over 1 inch of boiling water. Cover tightly and steam until crisp-tender, about 6 minutes. Transfer the asparagus to a plate. Add the carrot to the basket. Cover and steam until crisp-tender, 1–2 minutes.

2 **tablespoons** rice wine or dry sherry

1 **tablespoon** reduced-sodium soy sauce

1 **(1-inch) piece peeled** fresh ginger, minced

1 **garlic clove**, minced

½ **pound boneless top round** or sirloin steak, trimmed and cut into 2-inch strips

2 **teaspoons** peanut oil

1 **leek**, trimmed to white and light-green parts, cleaned, and thinly sliced

½ **teaspoon** hot chili paste (optional)

18 **fresh asparagus** spears, trimmed, cut into 3-inch pieces, and steamed

1 **carrot**, cut into thin strips and steamed

1 **teaspoon** cornstarch, dissolved in 1 tablespoon water

Dry-Cooked Shredded Beef

PREP 15 MINUTES PLUS 30 MINUTES MARINATING TIME
COOK ABOUT 10 MINUTES
SERVES 4

1 Combine the soy sauce, vinegar, and sesame oil in a zip-close plastic bag; add the steak. Squeeze out the air and seal the bag; turn to coat the steak. Refrigerate, turning the bag occasionally, at least 30 minutes. Drain the steak, reserving the marinade. Pat the steak dry with paper towels.

2 Whisk together the broth, cornstarch, Worcestershire sauce, honey, and crushed red pepper in a small bowl until smooth; set aside.

3 Heat a large nonstick skillet or wok over high heat until a drop of water sizzles. Add 2 teaspoons of the peanut oil, swirl to coat the pan, then add the steak. Stir-fry until lightly browned at the edges, 2–3 minutes. Transfer the steak to a plate and keep warm.

4 Add the remaining 1 teaspoon peanut oil to the skillet, swirl to coat the pan, then add the scallions, garlic, and ginger. Stir-fry until the scallions are softened, 1–2 minutes. Add the chili paste (if using) and stir-fry 5 seconds. Add the carrots, cabbage, and bean sprouts; stir-fry until the carrots are softened, 2–3 minutes. Add the reserved marinade and the broth mixture; cook until the sauce is slightly thickened, 1–2 minutes. Stir in the steak and cook, stirring gently, until heated through, 1–2 minutes. Sprinkle with the cilantro.

PER SERVING (1½ cups): 168 Cal, 8 g Fat, 2 g Sat Fat, 0 g Trans Fat, 33 mg Chol, 227 mg Sod, 11 g Carb, 2 g Fib, 15 g Prot, 34 mg Calc. **POINTS** value: *4.*

EXPRESS LANE To save time shredding the beef, pile several pieces on top of each other and cut lengthwise into thin strips.

Ingredients

- 1 tablespoon reduced-sodium soy sauce
- 1 teaspoon rice vinegar
- 1 teaspoon Asian (dark) sesame oil
- ½ pound boneless top round or sirloin steak, trimmed and cut into 2-inch strips
- ¼ cup reduced-sodium chicken broth
- 1 teaspoon cornstarch
- 1 teaspoon Worcestershire sauce
- 1 teaspoon honey
- Pinch crushed red pepper
- 3 teaspoons peanut oil
- 2 scallions, minced
- 1 garlic clove, minced
- ½ teaspoon minced peeled fresh ginger
- ½ teaspoon hot chili paste (optional)
- 2 carrots, shredded
- 1 cup thinly sliced green cabbage
- 1 cup bean sprouts
- 1 tablespoon minced fresh cilantro

Pork and Black Bean Stir-Fry

Pork and Black Bean Stir-Fry

PREP	15 MINUTES PLUS 1 HOUR MARINATING TIME
COOK	ABOUT 10 MINUTES
SERVES	4

1 Combine the soy sauce, sesame oil, ginger, and five-spice powder in a zip-close plastic bag; add the pork. Squeeze out the air and seal the bag; turn to coat the pork. Refrigerate, turning the bag occasionally, at least 1 hour. Drain the pork, reserving the marinade.

2 Heat a large nonstick skillet or wok over high heat until a drop of water sizzles. Add 1 teaspoon of the peanut oil, swirl to coat the pan, then add the pork. Stir-fry until just cooked through, 3–4 minutes. Transfer the pork to a plate and keep warm.

3 Add the remaining 1 teaspoon peanut oil to the skillet, swirl to coat the pan, then add the scallions, black beans, and garlic. Stir-fry until just fragrant, about 15 seconds. Add the mushrooms, leeks, and bell pepper; stir-fry until the mushrooms have released and reabsorbed their liquid and the bell pepper is softened, 4–5 minutes. Stir in the pork, the reserved marinade, and the dissolved cornstarch; cook until the sauce thickens and coats the pork, about 1 minute.

PER SERVING (about 1 cup): 168 Cal, 7 g Fat, 2 g Sat Fat, 0 g Trans Fat, 33 mg Chol, 301 mg Sod, 12 g Carb, 2 g Fib, 14 g Prot, 51 mg Calc. **POINTS** value: **4.**

TRY IT The secret to this delicious dish is Chinese fermented black beans. These are black beans that have been preserved in brine and dried. Their briny flavor is quite delicate, and they are often used in seafood and vegetable dishes. You can find fermented black beans in Asian markets, where they are usually quite inexpensive. Store them in an airtight plastic bag in the refrigerator; they'll keep up to a year. If unavailable, substitute 2 teaspoons black bean sauce.

- 1 tablespoon reduced-sodium soy sauce
- 1 teaspoon Asian (dark) sesame oil
- ½ teaspoon minced peeled fresh ginger
- ¼ teaspoon five-spice powder
- ½ pound boneless pork loin, trimmed and cut into 2-inch strips
- 2 teaspoons peanut oil
- 2 scallions, minced
- 1 tablespoon fermented black beans, rinsed, drained, and finely chopped
- 1 garlic clove, minced
- 2 cups sliced fresh mushrooms
- 2 leeks, trimmed to white and light-green parts, cleaned, and thinly sliced
- 1 red bell pepper, seeded and cut into thin strips
- 1 teaspoon cornstarch, dissolved in ⅓ cup water

Spicy Thai Beef Stir-Fry

PREP 20 MINUTES
COOK ABOUT 20 MINUTES
SERVES 4

1 Combine the broth, lime juice, coconut milk, brown sugar, cornstarch, fish sauce, sesame oil, and curry paste in a medium bowl; set aside.

2 Heat a large nonstick skillet or wok over high heat until a drop of water sizzles. Add 1 teaspoon of the peanut oil, swirl to coat the pan, then add the steak. Stir-fry in batches, until browned, about 4 minutes. Transfer each batch to a plate and set aside.

3 Add the remaining 1 teaspoon peanut oil to the skillet, swirl to coat the pan, then add the garlic and ginger. Stir-fry until fragrant, about 30 seconds. Add the bell peppers and stir-fry until crisp-tender, about 3 minutes. Add the watercress and stir-fry until it begins to wilt, about 3 minutes. Stir in the broth mixture and cook, stirring constantly, until the mixture boils and thickens, about 1 minute. Return the steak to the pan and toss to combine. Serve with the rice.

PER SERVING (1½ cups beef mixture with ½ cup rice): 366 Cal, 14 g Fat, 5 g Sat Fat, 1 g Trans Fat, 48 mg Chol, 260 mg Sod, 37 g Carb, 3 g Fib, 23 g Prot, 74 mg Calc. *POINTS* value: *8.*

GOOD IDEA To keep fresh ginger almost indefinitely, peel it, cut it into chunks, put in a small jar with enough dry sherry to cover, and stash it in the refrigerator. An added bonus: When the ginger is gone, you have ginger-infused sherry—delicious in salad dressings and stir-fries.

¾ **cup reduced-sodium chicken broth**

3 **tablespoons fresh lime juice**

3 **tablespoons coconut milk**

2 **tablespoons packed dark brown sugar**

1 **tablespoon cornstarch**

1 **tablespoon Thai fish sauce (nam pla)**

2 **teaspoons Asian (dark) sesame oil**

½ **teaspoon Thai green curry paste**

2 **teaspoons peanut oil**

¾ **pound flank steak, trimmed and cut into thin strips**

2 **garlic cloves, minced**

1 **teaspoon minced peeled fresh ginger**

2 **yellow bell peppers, seeded and cut into thin strips**

1 **bunch watercress, tough stems discarded (about 4 cups)**

2 **cups cooked brown rice**

Lo Mein Pork and Peanut Noodles

PREP 15 MINUTES
COOK ABOUT 25 MINUTES
SERVES 6

1 Combine ½ tablespoon of the soy sauce, 1 teaspoon of the ginger, and the sherry in a large bowl. Crush 1 of the garlic cloves through a garlic press.

2 Spray a large nonstick skillet or wok with nonstick spray and set over high heat. Add the pork and stir-fry until cooked through, about 5 minutes. Transfer the pork to the soy sauce mixture, toss to coat, and set aside.

3 Start to cook the noodles according to package directions. Meanwhile, to make the dressing, whisk together the broth, vinegar, brown sugar, peanut butter, curry paste, and the remaining 3 tablespoons soy sauce and ½ teaspoon ginger. Crush the remaining 2 garlic cloves through the press into the dressing. Drain the noodles and add them to the bowl with the pork, along with the bell pepper. Pour the dressing over and toss to coat.

4 Divide the lo mein among 6 bowls. Garnish each serving with the zucchini, scallions, and cilantro. Sprinkle with the peanuts (if using).

PER SERVING (1 ½ cups with ¼ teaspoon peanuts): 221 Cal, 5 g Fat, 1 g Sat Fat, 0 g Trans Fat, 25 mg Chol, 516 mg Sod, 32 g Carb, 3 g Fib, 15 g Prot, 23 mg Calc. *POINTS* value: *4.*

FOOD NOTE Instead of using the readily available thin Asian noodles labeled *lo mein* (loh MAYN) you could substitute any thin pasta, such as vermicelli or thin spaghetti.

3 ½ tablespoons reduced-sodium soy sauce

1 ½ teaspoons grated peeled fresh ginger

1 teaspoon dry sherry or rice wine

3 garlic cloves, peeled

½ pound pork tenderloin, trimmed and cut into matchstick-thin sticks

½ pound lo mein noodles

¼ cup chicken or vegetable broth

2 tablespoons rice vinegar

2 tablespoons packed light brown sugar

2 tablespoons reduced-fat peanut butter

½ teaspoon Thai red curry paste

1 large red bell pepper, seeded and cut into strips

1 small zucchini, cut into matchstick-thin sticks

3 scallions, thinly sliced

2 tablespoons chopped fresh cilantro

½ tablespoon chopped peanuts (optional)

Spicy Szechuan Chicken

PREP   20 MINUTES PLUS ABOUT 2 HOURS COOLING AND MARINATING TIME
COOK   ABOUT 15 MINUTES
SERVES 4

1 Toast the peppercorns in a small nonstick skillet over medium heat, shaking the skillet, until they begin to smoke, about 1 minute. Crush with a mortar and pestle or spice grinder. Sift through a fine sieve and discard the shells, reserving the powder.

2 Heat the same skillet over medium heat. Add the cinnamon and anise seeds; toast, stirring constantly, until fragrant and lightly browned, 45–60 seconds. Transfer to a plate and let cool.

3 Combine the peppercorn powder, cinnamon mixture, and sugar in a zip-close plastic bag; add the chicken. Squeeze out the air and seal the bag; shake well to coat the chicken. Refrigerate, turning the bag occasionally, at least 2 hours or overnight.

4 Heat a large nonstick skillet or wok over high heat until a drop of water sizzles. Add 1 teaspoon of the oil, swirl to coat the pan, then add the chicken. Stir-fry until cooked through, 1–2 minutes. Transfer the chicken to a plate and set aside.

5 Heat the remaining 1 teaspoon oil in the same skillet, swirl to coat the pan, then add the scallions and ginger. Stir-fry until the scallions are softened, about 2 minutes. Add the mushrooms and stir-fry until they have released and reabsorbed their liquid, 3–4 minutes. Add the bok choy and stir-fry until wilted, about 3 minutes. Add the chicken, water chestnuts, and soy sauce; cook, stirring gently, until heated through, 3–4 minutes.

- ½ teaspoon Szechuan peppercorns
- 1 teaspoon cinnamon
- ½ teaspoon anise seeds
- 1 teaspoon sugar
- 10 ounces skinless boneless chicken breasts, cut into thin strips
- 2 teaspoons peanut oil
- 4 scallions, thinly sliced
- 1 (½-inch) piece peeled fresh ginger, minced
- 2 cups thinly sliced fresh mushrooms
- 4 cups thinly sliced bok choy
- ¾ cup water chestnuts, coarsely chopped
- 1 tablespoon reduced-sodium soy sauce

PER SERVING (about 1¼ cups): 152 Cal, 3 g Fat, 1 g Sat Fat, 0 g Trans Fat, 41 mg Chol, 248 mg Sod, 11 g Carb, 1 g Fib, 19 g Prot, 101 mg Calc. *POINTS* value: *3*.

Spicy Szechuan Chicken

Chicken Chow Mein

PREP 10 MINUTES
COOK ABOUT 10 MINUTES
SERVES 4

1 Whisk together the broth, cornstarch, soy sauce, and sugar in a small bowl until smooth; set aside.

2 Heat a large nonstick skillet or wok over high heat until a drop of water sizzles. Add the oil, swirl to coat the pan, then add the scallions, ginger, and garlic. Stir-fry until the scallions are softened, about 2 minutes. Add the celery and bell pepper; stir-fry until softened, about 5 minutes. Add the bean sprouts and stir-fry until softened, about 1 minute. Add the chicken and the broth mixture; cook, stirring gently, until the sauce thickens and coats the chicken, 1–2 minutes. Transfer to a platter and serve with the noodles.

PER SERVING (about 1½ cups): 173 Cal, 6 g Fat, 1 g Sat Fat, 0 g Trans Fat, 36 mg Chol, 262 mg Sod, 14 g Carb, 1 g Fib, 16 g Prot, 28 mg Calc. **POINTS** value: **4.**

FOOD NOTE Chow mein noodles aren't just for stir-fry dishes. They also make a wonderful crunchy garnish sprinkled atop Chinese chicken salad or any tossed green salad with an Asian-style dressing (¼ cup noodles have a **POINTS** value of 1½).

½ cup reduced-sodium chicken broth

1 tablespoon cornstarch

1 tablespoon reduced-sodium soy sauce

1 teaspoon sugar

1 teaspoon peanut oil

4 scallions, thinly sliced

1 (½-inch) piece peeled fresh ginger, minced

1 garlic clove, minced

2 celery stalks, thinly sliced

½ red bell pepper, seeded and diced

1 cup bean sprouts

1½ cups shredded cooked chicken breast

1 cup chow mein noodles

Kung Pao Chicken

PREP　15 MINUTES PLUS 30 MINUTES MARINATING TIME
COOK　ABOUT 5 MINUTES
SERVES　4

1 Whisk together the egg white, cornstarch, and salt in a medium bowl until smooth; add the chicken and stir to coat. Refrigerate, covered, about 30 minutes.

2 Combine the water, hoisin sauce, vinegar, soy sauce, sugar, chili paste, and garlic in a small bowl; set aside.

3 Heat a large nonstick skillet or wok over high heat until a drop of water sizzles. Add 1 teaspoon of the oil, swirl to coat the pan, then add the chile peppers. Stir-fry until blackened, about 1 minute. With a slotted spoon, transfer the chile peppers to a plate.

4 Heat the remaining 1 teaspoon oil in the skillet. Add the chicken mixture and stir-fry until the chicken is cooked through (do not brown), 1–2 minutes. Transfer the chicken to a plate and keep warm.

5 Add the hoisin mixture to the skillet and cook, stirring constantly, until fragrant, about 30 seconds. Stir in the chicken, chile peppers, and broccoli; cook, stirring gently, until heated through, 2–3 minutes. Sprinkle with the peanuts.

PER SERVING (about 1 cup): 195 Cal, 7 g Fat, 1 g Sat Fat, 0 g Trans Fat, 37 mg Chol, 309 mg Sod, 13 g Carb, 4 g Fib, 21 g Prot, 58 mg Calc. **POINTS** value: **4.**

TRY IT Chinese hot chili paste is a pungent condiment made from mashed red-hot chile peppers, vinegar, and seasonings (often including garlic). Stored in the refrigerator, it will keep over a year, but its potency decreases as it ages. Find it in Asian markets and gourmet grocery stores. If unavailable, substitute ¼ teaspoon crushed red pepper.

1 egg white

2 teaspoons cornstarch

Pinch salt

½ pound skinless boneless chicken breasts, cut into ¾-inch cubes

3 tablespoons water

1 tablespoon hoisin sauce

1 tablespoon rice vinegar

2 teaspoons reduced-sodium soy sauce

1 teaspoon sugar

½ teaspoon hot chili paste

1 garlic clove, minced

2 teaspoons peanut oil

4 dried Szechuan chile peppers, seeds removed

3 cups fresh broccoli florets, steamed

¼ cup unsalted dry-roasted peanuts, coarsely chopped

Moo Shu Turkey

Moo Shu Turkey

PREP   20 MINUTES PLUS ABOUT 1 HOUR MARINATING AND STANDING TIME
COOK   ABOUT 15 MINUTES
SERVES 4

1 Combine 1 tablespoon of the soy sauce, the sugar, and Worcestershire sauce in a zip-close plastic bag; add the turkey. Seal the bag; turn to coat the turkey. Refrigerate, turning the bag occasionally, at least 30 minutes. Drain the turkey, reserving the marinade.

2 Meanwhile, bring the water to a boil in a small saucepan. Add the mushrooms and fungi, cover, and remove from the heat. Let stand until softened, about 20 minutes. Drain, discarding the liquid; thinly slice the mushrooms and cut the fungi into ½-inch-thick strips.

3 Heat a large nonstick skillet or wok over high heat. Add 1 teaspoon of the oil, swirl to coat the pan, then add the turkey. Stir-fry until cooked through, 2–3 minutes. Transfer the turkey to a plate and keep warm.

4 Heat 1 teaspoon of the oil in the skillet, swirl to coat the pan, then add the egg whites. Stir-fry until scrambled, about 1 minute. Transfer the egg whites to the plate with the turkey and keep warm.

5 Heat the remaining 1 teaspoon oil in the skillet. Add the cabbage, bell pepper, mushrooms, and fungi; stir-fry until tender, 6–8 minutes. Stir in the bean sprouts, vinegar, the remaining 1 tablespoon soy sauce, and the reserved marinade; cook 1 minute. Stir in the turkey and egg whites; toss gently to combine.

6 Spread each tortilla with 1 teaspoon of the hoisin sauce; spoon the turkey mixture into the center and fold over to enclose the filling.

PER SERVING (1 tortilla with about ½ cup filling): 254 Cal, 4 g Fat, 1 g Sat Fat, 0 g Trans Fat, 31 mg Chol, 743 mg Sod, 33 g Carb, 3 g Fib, 20 g Prot, 67 mg Calc. **POINTS** value: **5.**

2 tablespoons reduced-sodium soy sauce

1 teaspoon sugar

½ teaspoon Worcestershire sauce

½ pound skinless boneless turkey breast, cut into thin strips

1 cup water

5 dried Chinese black mushroom caps (about ½ ounce)

½ ounce dried Chinese "tree ear" fungi

3 teaspoons peanut oil

3 egg whites, lightly beaten

1 cup shredded napa cabbage

½ red bell pepper, seeded and cut into thin strips

1 cup bean sprouts

1 tablespoon rice vinegar

4 (6-inch) flour tortillas

2 tablespoons + 2 teaspoons hoisin sauce

Singapore Noodles

PREP   20 MINUTES
COOK ABOUT 25 MINUTES
SERVES 4

1 Cook the spaghettini according to package directions omitting the salt, if desired; drain. Rinse the spaghettini under warm running water; drain and transfer to a large serving bowl. Add the sesame oil and toss lightly; keep warm.

2 Whisk together the broth, cornstarch, cinnamon, and coconut extract in a small bowl until smooth; set aside.

3 Heat a large nonstick skillet or wok over high heat until a drop of water sizzles. Add 2 teaspoons of the peanut oil, swirl to coat the pan, then add the curry powder. Stir-fry until just fragrant, about 30 seconds. Add the shrimp and stir-fry until just opaque in the center, 2–3 minutes. Transfer to a plate and keep warm.

4 Add the remaining 1 teaspoon peanut oil to the skillet, swirl to coat the pan, then add the onion. Stir-fry until softened, about 5 minutes. Stir in the broth mixture, the carrot, peas, and spinach; cook until the spinach wilts and the sauce is slightly thickened, about 1 minute. Add to the spaghettini with the shrimp; toss to coat.

PER SERVING (about 1½ cups): 291 Cal, 8 g Fat, 1 g Sat Fat, 0 g Trans Fat, 116 mg Chol, 198 mg Sod, 36 g Carb, 4 g Fib, 20 g Prot, 90 mg Calc. *POINTS* value: *6.*

HOW WE DID IT To prep the shrimp, with kitchen scissors or a small knife, cut the shrimp shell along the outer curve, just deep enough to expose the dark vein. Peel back the shell and gently separate the shell from the shrimp; discard. Remove the vein with the tip of a small knife; discard. Rinse the shrimp under cold running water.

¼ **pound** spaghettini

1 **teaspoon** Asian (dark) sesame oil

1 **cup** reduced-sodium chicken broth

2 **teaspoons** cornstarch

½ **teaspoon** cinnamon

¼ **teaspoon** coconut extract

3 **teaspoons** peanut oil

1 **tablespoon** curry powder

½ **pound** medium shrimp, **peeled and deveined**

½ **onion, diced**

1 **carrot, diced and steamed**

1 **cup thawed frozen peas**

1 **cup chopped cleaned fresh spinach**

Five-Treasure Rice

PREP 15 MINUTES
COOK ABOUT 10 MINUTES
SERVES 4

1 Whisk together the broth, soy sauce, wine, cornstarch, white pepper, and five-spice powder (if using) in a small bowl until smooth; set aside.

2 Place the rice in a shallow bowl. With moistened fingers, stir the rice to separate the grains.

3 Heat a large nonstick skillet or wok over high heat until a drop of water sizzles. Add the oil, swirl to coat the pan, then add the scallions and ginger. Stir-fry until the scallions are softened, 2–3 minutes. Add the peas, shrimp, chicken, egg whites, and the broth mixture; stir-fry until the egg whites are cooked, about 3 minutes. Stir in the rice and cook, tossing gently, until heated through, 2–3 minutes. Sprinkle with the walnuts.

PER SERVING (about 1½ cups): 259 Cal, 8 g Fat, 1 g Sat Fat, 0 g Trans Fat, 67 mg Chol, 299 mg Sod, 28 g Carb, 2 g Fib, 17 g Prot, 44 mg Calc. **POINTS** value: **5.**

HOW WE DID IT To toast the walnuts, preheat the oven to 350°F. Spread the walnuts in a shallow baking pan; bake, stirring as needed, until golden brown, 8 to 10 minutes.

2 tablespoons reduced-sodium chicken broth

1 tablespoon reduced-sodium soy sauce

1 tablespoon rice wine or dry sherry

1 teaspoon cornstarch

Pinch ground white pepper

Pinch five-spice powder (optional)

2 cups cold cooked long-grain white or brown rice

2 teaspoons peanut oil

4 scallions, sliced

1 (½-inch) piece peeled fresh ginger, minced

1 cup thawed frozen peas

¼ pound small shrimp, cooked and peeled

½ cup shredded cooked chicken breast

2 egg whites, beaten

¼ cup walnuts, toasted

Shrimp Fried Rice

PREP 15 MINUTES
COOK ABOUT 10 MINUTES
SERVES 4

1 Whisk together the egg and egg whites in a small bowl until frothy; set aside.

2 Place the rice in a shallow bowl. With moistened fingers, stir the rice to separate the grains.

3 Heat a large nonstick skillet or wok over high heat until a drop of water sizzles. Add 1 teaspoon of the oil, swirl to coat the pan, then add the shrimp and ham. Stir-fry until the shrimp just turn barely pink, 30–60 seconds. Transfer the shrimp and ham to a plate.

4 Add the remaining 1 teaspoon oil to the skillet, swirl to coat the pan, then add the scallions and bell pepper. Stir-fry until softened, about 5 minutes. Add the rice and stir-fry until heated through, about 1 minute.

5 Make a well in the center of the rice and add the egg mixture, stirring the eggs constantly, until they are soft-scrambled, about 1 minute. Immediately start incorporating the rice mixture, stirring in a circular motion. When thoroughly blended, add the peas and stir-fry 1 minute. Add the bean sprouts, the shrimp mixture, and the oyster sauce; cook, tossing lightly, until the bean sprouts are tender, about 2 minutes.

PER SERVING (1½ cups): 267 Cal, 5 g Fat, 1 g Sat Fat, 0 g Trans Fat, 143 mg Chol, 433 mg Sod, 33 g Carb, 2 g Fib, 21 g Prot, 67 mg Calc. **POINTS** value: **5.**

TRY IT To accentuate the seafood flavor of the dish, we added oyster sauce—a rich, deeply flavored, cured condiment made from oysters, salt, soy sauce, and other seasonings. Look for it at the supermarket or an Asian market.

- 1 large **egg**
- 2 **egg whites**
- 2½ cups cold **cooked white rice**
- 2 teaspoons **peanut oil**
- ½ pound **small shrimp, peeled and deveined**
- ¼ cup **diced ham**
- 8 **scallions, thinly sliced**
- ½ **red bell pepper, seeded and diced**
- ½ cup **thawed frozen peas**
- 1 cup **bean sprouts**
- 1 tablespoon **oyster sauce**

Shrimp Egg Fu Yung

Shrimp Egg Fu Yung

PREP 10 MINUTES PLUS ABOUT 15 MINUTES COOLING TIME
COOK ABOUT 15 MINUTES
SERVES 4

1 Heat the oil a medium nonstick skillet over medium-high heat. Add the ginger and cook, stirring constantly, until just fragrant, about 15 seconds. Add the mushrooms and scallions; cook, stirring frequently, until the mushrooms have released and reabsorbed their liquid and the scallions are softened, 6–8 minutes. Stir in the bean sprouts, soy sauce, and sugar; cook until heated through, about 1 minute. Let cool.

2 Beat the eggs and egg whites in a large bowl until frothy. Stir in the cooked vegetables and the shrimp.

3 Spray the skillet with nonstick spray and set over medium-high heat. Add one-fourth of the egg mixture, tilting to cover the bottom of the pan. Cook until the underside is set, 45–60 seconds. Turn over and cook until lightly browned, 30–45 seconds. Slide the omelette onto a plate and keep warm. Repeat 3 times with the remaining egg mixture, spraying the skillet each time with nonstick spray.

4 Whisk together the broth, wine, Worcestershire sauce, and cornstarch in a medium saucepan until smooth; bring to a boil. Reduce the heat and simmer, stirring occasionally, until thickened, 1–2 minutes. Pour the sauce over the omelettes and sprinkle with the cilantro.

PER SERVING (1 omelette with about 1 tablespoon sauce): 174 Cal, 7 g Fat, 2 g Sat Fat, 0 g Trans Fat, 270 mg Chol, 384 mg Sod, 7 g Carb, 1 g Fib, 21 g Prot, 59 mg Calc. **POINTS** value: **4.**

EXPRESS LANE The omelettes can be refrigerated overnight; reheat in a 350°F oven about 10 minutes. The sauce should always be freshly prepared.

1 **teaspoon** peanut oil

½ **teaspoon minced peeled** fresh ginger

1 **cup sliced** fresh shiitake mushrooms

8 **scallions, thinly sliced**

1 **cup** bean sprouts

1 **tablespoon** reduced-sodium soy sauce

1 **teaspoon** sugar

3 **large eggs**

3 **egg whites**

¼ **pound cooked peeled small shrimp, chopped**

¼ **cup** reduced-sodium chicken broth

1 **tablespoon** rice wine or dry sherry

½ **teaspoon** Worcestershire sauce

1 **teaspoon** cornstarch

1 **tablespoon minced fresh** cilantro

Sweet-and-Sour Shrimp

PREP   15 MINUTES
COOK   ABOUT 10 MINUTES
SERVES 4

1 Whisk together the pineapple juice, sugar, vinegar, tomato paste, soy sauce, cornstarch, and pepper sauce in a medium bowl until smooth; set aside.

2 Heat a large nonstick skillet or wok over high heat until a drop of water sizzles. Add 2 teaspoons of the oil, swirl to coat the pan, then add the shrimp. Stir-fry until just opaque in the center, 3–4 minutes. Transfer the shrimp to a bowl and set aside.

3 Add the remaining 1 teaspoon oil to the skillet, swirl to coat the pan, then add the ginger and garlic. Stir-fry until just fragrant, about 30 seconds. Add the carrots, onion, bell pepper, and bamboo shoots; stir-fry until the vegetables begin to soften, 4–5 minutes. Stir in the shrimp and the pineapple juice mixture. Bring to a boil and cook, stirring occasionally, until thickened, about 2 minutes. Sprinkle with the peanuts.

PER SERVING (1¼ cups): 358 Cal, 11 g Fat, 1 g Sat Fat, 0 g Trans Fat, 210 mg Chol, 439 mg Sod, 33 g Carb, 4 g Fib, 33 g Prot, 112 mg Calc. *POINTS* value: *7.*

FOOD NOTE Since the shrimp in this classic recipe are stir-fried in a modest amount of oil, we've added peanuts for extra flavor and crunch. (Or skip the nuts and reduce the per-serving *POINTS* value by 1.)

¾ cup pineapple juice

3 tablespoons sugar

3 tablespoons rice vinegar

2 tablespoons tomato paste

1 tablespoon reduced-sodium soy sauce

1 tablespoon cornstarch

2 dashes hot pepper sauce

3 teaspoons vegetable oil

1½ pounds medium shrimp, peeled and deveined

1 tablespoon grated peeled fresh ginger

2 garlic cloves, minced

2 carrots, very thinly sliced

1 onion, chopped

1 green bell pepper, seeded and chopped

1 (8-ounce) can bamboo shoots, drained

¼ cup dry-roasted peanuts

Shrimp with "Lobster" Sauce

PREP 10 MINUTES
COOK ABOUT 10 MINUTES
SERVES 4

1 Heat a large nonstick skillet or wok over high heat until a drop of water sizzles. Add 1 teaspoon of the oil, swirl to coat the pan, then add the shrimp. Stir-fry until just opaque in the center, 2–3 minutes. Transfer to a plate and keep warm.

2 Add the remaining 1 teaspoon oil to the skillet, swirl to coat the pan, then add the black beans and garlic. Stir-fry until just fragrant, about 15 seconds. Add the scallions and stir-fry until the scallions are very soft, about 5 minutes. Stir in the shrimp, broth, the dissolved cornstarch, the wine, soy sauce, and sugar; bring to a boil and cook, stirring occasionally, until the sauce is slightly thickened, about 1 minute. Remove from the heat and add the egg whites, pouring in a thin stream around the sides of the skillet. Cook, stirring, until the egg whites are cooked through, about 1 minute more.

PER SERVING (about 1 cup): 144 Cal, 4 g Fat, 1 g Sat Fat, 0 g Trans Fat, 129 mg Chol, 424 mg Sod, 5 g Carb, 0 g Fib, 20 g Prot, 62 mg Calc. **POINTS** value: **3.**

FOOD NOTE Looking over this recipe, you might wonder, "Where's the lobster?" This classic dish is so named because the shrimp are cooked in a black bean sauce traditionally used on lobster.

2 teaspoons peanut oil

¾ pound medium shrimp, peeled and deveined

1 tablespoon fermented black beans, rinsed, drained, and finely chopped

1 garlic clove, minced

8 scallions, thinly sliced

⅓ cup reduced-sodium chicken broth

2 teaspoons cornstarch, dissolved in 2 tablespoons water

1 tablespoon rice wine or dry sherry

1 tablespoon reduced-sodium soy sauce

½ teaspoon sugar

2 egg whites, beaten

Spicy Soft-Shell Crabs

PREP	10 MINUTES
COOK	ABOUT 10 MINUTES
SERVES	4

1 Whisk together the water, wine, soy sauce, cornstarch, and sugar in a small bowl until smooth; set aside.

2 Heat 1 tablespoon of the oil in a large nonstick skillet over medium-high heat. Add 4 of the crabs, shell-side down, and cook until their shells turn reddish brown, 1–2 minutes. Turn over with a spatula or tongs and cook until browned, 1–2 minutes. Transfer to a plate and keep warm; repeat with the remaining crabs.

3 Heat the remaining 1 teaspoon oil in the skillet. Add the ginger and garlic; cook, stirring constantly, until just fragrant, about 15 seconds. Add the scallions and black beans; cook, stirring frequently, until the scallions are softened, 3–4 minutes. Add the crabs and the wine mixture; cook, stirring gently, until the sauce thickens and coats the crabs, about 2 minutes.

PER SERVING (2 crabs): 201 Cal, 6 g Fat, 1 g Sat Fat, 0 g Trans Fat, 135 mg Chol, 639 mg Sod, 5 g Carb, 0 g Fib, 28 g Prot, 17 mg Calc. **POINTS** value: *5.*

PLAY IT SAFE Soft-shell crabs are highly perishable, so buy them live, have your fishmonger clean them for you, and cook them within 4 hours of purchasing. These tasty morsels used to be a delicacy relegated only to the late spring and early summer, when crabs shed their shells—making this dish a wonderful way to welcome the warmer weather.

¼ cup water

1 tablespoon rice wine or dry sherry

1 tablespoon reduced-sodium soy sauce

1 teaspoon cornstarch

1 teaspoon packed dark brown sugar

1 tablespoon + 1 teaspoon peanut oil

8 small (3-ounce) soft-shell crabs, cleaned

1 (½-inch) piece peeled fresh ginger, minced

1 garlic clove, minced

8 scallions, cut into 2-inch lengths

1 tablespoon fermented black beans, rinsed, drained, and finely chopped

Spicy Soft-Shell Crabs

Vegetable Lo Mein

Vegetable Lo Mein

PREP   15 MINUTES PLUS 20 MINUTES STANDING TIME
COOK   ABOUT 30 MINUTES
SERVES 4

1 Bring 1 cup water to a boil in a small saucepan. Add the mushrooms, cover, and remove from the heat. Let stand until softened, about 20 minutes. Drain, discarding the liquid, and thinly slice.

2 Meanwhile, cook the noodles according to package directions omitting the salt, if desired; drain. Rinse the noodles under warm running water; drain and transfer to a medium bowl. Add the sesame oil and toss lightly.

3 Combine the hoisin sauce, soy sauce, vinegar, crushed red pepper, and 3 tablespoons water in a small bowl; set aside.

4 Heat a large nonstick skillet or wok over high heat until a drop of water sizzles. Add the peanut oil, swirl to coat the pan, then add the ginger and garlic. Stir-fry until just fragrant, about 15 seconds. Add the scallions, bell pepper, and celery; stir-fry until the vegetables are softened, 5–8 minutes. Add the bok choy, bamboo shoots, and mushrooms; cook, stirring gently, until the bok choy is wilted, 3–4 minutes. Stir in the noodles and hoisin mixture; cook, stirring gently, until the noodles have absorbed the sauce, 2–3 minutes. Sprinkle with the peanuts and cilantro.

PER SERVING (about 1½ cups): 225 Cal, 7 g Fat, 1 g Sat Fat, 0 g Trans Fat, 30 mg Chol, 270 mg Sod, 33 g Carb, 4 g Fib, 8 g Prot, 71 mg Calc. **POINTS** value: **4.**

TRY IT Dried Chinese black mushroom caps provide a smoky, meat-like flavor to many vegetarian dishes. The mushrooms can be found in Asian markets and can be stored in an airtight bag for up to 1 year.

5 **dried Chinese black mushroom caps (about ½ ounce)**

¼ **pound thin egg noodle clusters or fideos**

1 teaspoon **Asian (dark) sesame oil**

1 tablespoon **hoisin sauce**

1 tablespoon **reduced-sodium soy sauce**

1 tablespoon **rice vinegar**

Pinch **crushed red pepper**

1 teaspoon **peanut oil**

1 (½-inch) piece peeled **fresh ginger, minced**

1 **garlic clove, minced**

8 **scallions, thinly sliced**

½ **red bell pepper, cut into thin strips**

1 **celery stalk, sliced**

2 cups thinly sliced **bok choy**

½ **cup canned sliced bamboo shoots**

¼ **cup dry-roasted peanuts, chopped**

2 tablespoons minced **fresh cilantro**

Buddha's Delight

PREP 15 MINUTES PLUS 20 MINUTES STANDING TIME
COOK ABOUT 20 MINUTES
SERVES 4

1 Bring 1 cup water to a boil in a small saucepan. Add the mushrooms and fungi, cover, and remove from the heat. Let stand until softened, about 20 minutes. Drain, discarding the liquid; thinly slice the mushrooms and cut the fungi into ½-inch-thick strips.

2 Meanwhile, whisk together the soy sauce, vinegar, hoisin sauce, cornstarch, and ¼ cup water in a small bowl until smooth; set aside.

3 Heat a large nonstick skillet or wok over high heat. Add 1 teaspoon of the oil, swirl to coat the pan, then add the wheat gluten. Stir-fry until lightly browned, 3–4 minutes. Transfer to a plate and keep warm.

4 Add the remaining 1 teaspoon oil to the skillet, swirl to coat the pan, then add the garlic and ginger. Stir-fry until just fragrant, about 15 seconds. Add the scallions and stir-fry until softened, 3–4 minutes. Stir in the bok choy, carrot, and ¼ cup water; cook, stirring occasionally, until the carrot is tender and most of the liquid evaporates, 8–10 minutes. Stir in the wheat gluten, baby corn, bean sprouts, bamboo shoots, mushrooms, and fungi; stir-fry about 1 minute. Stir in the soy sauce mixture; cook, stirring gently, until the sauce is thickened, about 2 minutes.

PER SERVING (about 1½ cups): 132 Cal, 3 g Fat, 0 g Sat Fat, 0 g Trans Fat, 0 mg Chol, 259 mg Sod, 19 g Carb, 6 g Fib, 8 g Prot, 93 mg Calc. **POINTS** value: **2.**

GOOD IDEA If you can't find wheat gluten in an Asian market or natural-foods store, substitute firm tofu that has been pressed in a cheesecloth-lined sieve for several hours to remove its moisture.

5 dried Chinese black mushroom caps (about ½ ounce)

½ ounce dried Chinese "tree ear" fungi

1 tablespoon reduced-sodium soy sauce

2 teaspoons rice vinegar

2 teaspoons hoisin sauce

1 teaspoon cornstarch

2 teaspoons peanut oil

¼ pound wheat gluten, rinsed and sliced

1 garlic clove, minced

½ teaspoon minced peeled fresh ginger

8 scallions, thinly sliced

2 cups sliced bok choy

1 carrot, cut into thin strips

1 cup drained rinsed canned baby corn

1 cup bean sprouts

½ cup drained rinsed canned sliced bamboo shoots

Pad Thai

PREP 10 MINUTES PLUS 20 MINUTES STANDING TIME
COOK ABOUT 25 MINUTES
SERVES 4

1 Cook the vermicelli according to package directions omitting the salt, if desired; drain and keep warm.

2 Meanwhile, bring the water to a boil in a small saucepan. Add the mushrooms, cover, and remove from the heat. Let stand until softened, about 20 minutes. Drain, discarding the liquid, and thinly slice.

3 Heat a large nonstick skillet or wok over high heat until a drop of water sizzles. Add the oil, swirl to coat the pan, then add the scallions and garlic. Stir-fry until the scallions are softened, 3–4 minutes. Add the chili paste and stir-fry until fragrant, about 10 seconds. Add the lime juice, soy sauce, and sugar; cook, stirring, until the sugar dissolves, about 30 seconds.

4 Add the mushrooms and cook until they have absorbed some of the sauce, about 1 minute. Stir in the egg whites and cook, stirring gently, until they begin to set, about 30 seconds. Add the vermicelli and bean sprouts; cook, stirring gently, until mixed and heated through, 2–3 minutes. Sprinkle with the peanuts and garnish with the cilantro (if using).

PER SERVING (about 1 cup): 246 Cal, 7 g Fat, 1 g Sat Fat, 0 g Trans Fat, 0 mg Chol, 370 mg Sod, 41 g Carb, 3 g Fib, 7 g Prot, 35 mg Calc. **POINTS** value: **5.**

¼ **pound** vermicelli or spaghetti

1 **cup** water

10 **dried Chinese black mushroom caps (about 1 ounce)**

2 **teaspoons vegetable oil**

8 **scallions, minced**

1 **garlic clove, minced**

1 **teaspoon hot chili paste**

¼ **cup fresh lime juice**

2 **tablespoons reduced-sodium soy sauce**

1 **tablespoon sugar**

3 **egg whites**

1 **cup bean sprouts**

¼ **cup unsalted dry-roasted peanuts, chopped**

Fresh cilantro leaves, for garnish (optional)

FOOD NOTE If you're looking for true authenticity, try rice noodles instead of the vermicelli: They need to be soaked in warm water for about 20 minutes, then drained. Add them to soups or other stir-fried dishes as well.

Broccoli in Oyster Sauce

PREP 10 MINUTES
COOK ABOUT 15 MINUTES
SERVES 4

1 Whisk together the oyster sauce, water, soy sauce, vinegar, cornstarch, sugar, and sesame oil in a small bowl until smooth; set aside.

2 Heat a large nonstick skillet or wok over high heat until a drop of water sizzles. Add the peanut oil, swirl to coat the pan, then add the scallions, ginger, and garlic. Stir-fry until the scallions are softened, 1–2 minutes. Add the broccoli and stir-fry about 1 minute. Stir in the oyster sauce mixture; cook, stirring gently, until the sauce thickens and coats the broccoli, about 1 minute.

PER SERVING (about 1 cup): 70 Cal, 3 g Fat, 0 g Sat Fat, 0 g Trans Fat, 0 mg Chol, 532 mg Sod, 10 g Carb, 3 g Fib, 4 g Prot, 52 mg Calc. **POINTS** value: *1.*

GOOD IDEA Once you've mastered this classic recipe, try it with any vegetable—green beans, bok choy, cauliflower, and mushrooms are all good choices.

2 tablespoons oyster sauce

2 tablespoons water

1 tablespoon reduced-sodium soy sauce

1 tablespoon rice vinegar

2 teaspoons cornstarch

1 teaspoon sugar

1 teaspoon Asian (dark) sesame oil

1 teaspoon peanut oil

4 scallions, thinly sliced

½ teaspoon minced peeled fresh ginger

1 garlic clove, minced

4 cups fresh broccoli florets and stems, sliced into 2-inch pieces and steamed

15-Minute Meals

CHAPTER 2

Steak with Spicy Chili Sauce

PREP 5 MINUTES
COOK ABOUT 10 MINUTES
SERVES 4

1 Combine the vinegar, brown sugar, shallots, chili paste, garlic, 1 teaspoon of the oil, and ¼ teaspoon of the salt in a large bowl. Add the steaks, turning to coat. Remove the steaks, reserving the sauce; pat the steaks lightly with paper towels and sprinkle with the remaining ½ teaspoon salt.

2 Heat the remaining ½ teaspoon oil in a large nonstick skillet over high heat until almost smoking. Add the steaks in a single layer so that they don't touch, and cook until medium-rare, about 4 minutes on each side. Transfer the steaks to a plate and keep warm.

3 Add the reserved sauce to the pan. Bring to a boil over medium-high heat and cook, stirring occasionally, until thick and syrupy, about 3 minutes. Spoon the sauce over the steaks.

PER SERVING (1 steak with about 3 tablespoons sauce): 234 Cal, 10 g Fat, 3 g Sat Fat, 2 g Trans Fat, 57 mg Chol, 600 mg Sod, 12 g Carb, 0 g Fib, 24 g Prot, 19 mg Calc. ***POINTS*** value: **6.**

½ cup red-wine vinegar

3 tablespoons packed light brown sugar

2 shallots, minced

1 tablespoon Thai red chili paste

1 garlic clove, minced

1½ teaspoons vegetable oil

¾ teaspoon salt

4 (¼-pound) beef tenderloin steaks, 1-inch thick, trimmed

GOOD IDEA This dish would be fabulous with a side of mashed sweet potatoes (⅔ cup for each serving would increase the ***POINTS*** value by 2).

Hoisin Pork Stir-Fry

PREP 5 MINUTES
COOK ABOUT 10 MINUTES
SERVES 4

1 Cook the rice according to package directions omitting the salt, if desired.

2 Meanwhile, combine the pork, sherry, soy sauce, and cornstarch in a large bowl; set aside.

3 Heat a large nonstick skillet or wok over high heat until a drop of water sizzles. Add the sesame oil, swirl to coat the pan, then add the broccoli and bell pepper. Stir-fry until crisp-tender, about 2 minutes. Add the pork mixture and stir-fry until browned, about 4 minutes. Add the orange juice, hoisin sauce, and honey; cook, stirring frequently, until the pork is cooked through, about 2 minutes. Serve with the rice.

PER SERVING (1 cup pork mixture with ½ cup rice): 313 Cal, 6 g Fat, 2 g Sat Fat, 0 Trans Fat, 54 mg Chol, 453 mg Sod, 43 g Carb, 3 g Fib, 22 g Prot, 51 mg Calc. **POINTS** value: **6.**

GOOD IDEA Try this tasty no-**POINTS** value cucumber salad to set off this stir-fry in style. Just pull out your food processor to mince 1 small red onion. Remove the onion, then fit the processor with a fine slicing disk and slice 2 large peeled cucumbers. Add the cucumbers to the onion and drizzle with 2 or 3 tablespoons of rice-wine vinegar.

1½ cups quick-cooking white rice

¾ pound boneless pork loin, trimmed and cut into thin strips

2 tablespoons dry sherry

1 tablespoon reduced-sodium soy sauce

1 tablespoon cornstarch

1 teaspoon Asian (dark) sesame oil

2 cups fresh broccoli florets

1 red bell pepper, seeded and chopped

¼ cup orange juice

¼ cup hoisin sauce

2 tablespoons honey

Ginger-Pork Stir-Fry

Ginger-Pork Stir-Fry

PREP 10 MINUTES INCLUDING STANDING TIME
COOK ABOUT 5 MINUTES
SERVES 4

1 Whisk together the broth, oyster sauce, and cornstarch in a small bowl until smooth; set aside.

2 Place the noodles in a medium bowl with enough hot water to cover the noodles. Let stand until softened, about 10 minutes. Drain and place on a serving platter; keep warm.

3 Meanwhile, heat a large nonstick skillet or wok over high heat until a drop of water sizzles. Add the peanut oil, swirl to coat the pan, then add the snow peas, bell pepper, and ginger. Stir-fry until softened, 2–3 minutes. Transfer to a plate and keep warm.

4 Add the sesame oil to the skillet, swirl to coat the pan, then add the pork. Stir-fry until heated through, about 1 minute. Add the broth mixture and cook, stirring constantly, until the sauce thickens and coats the pork, 1–2 minutes. Place the vegetables over the noodles; top with the pork and sauce.

PER SERVING (1¾ cups): 281 Cal, 10 g Fat, 3 g Sat Fat, 0 g Trans Fat, 46 mg Chol, 228 mg Sod, 27 g Carb, 3 g Fib, 19 g Prot, 52 mg Calc. **POINTS** value: **6.**

½ cup **reduced-sodium chicken broth**

1 tablespoon **oyster sauce**

1 teaspoon **cornstarch**

¼ pound **cellophane noodles**

1 tablespoon **peanut oil**

2 cups trimmed **fresh snow peas**

1 **red bell pepper,** seeded and cut into thin strips

1 tablespoon chopped peeled **fresh ginger**

1 teaspoon **Asian (dark) sesame oil**

2 cups cubed **cooked lean pork**

Pineapple Pork Sauté

PREP 5 MINUTES
COOK ABOUT 10 MINUTES
SERVES 4

1 Cook the rice according to package directions omitting the salt, if desired.

2 Meanwhile, sprinkle the pork with the salt and ground pepper. Spray a large nonstick skillet with nonstick spray and set over medium-high heat. Add the pork in a single layer and cook, in batches if necessary, until browned, 1–2 minutes on each side. Transfer the pork to a plate.

3 Heat the oil in the skillet. Add the scallions, apple, bell pepper, garlic, and crushed red pepper; cook, stirring occasionally, until tender, about 5 minutes. Stir in the pineapple, sweet-and-sour sauce, and the pork; bring to a boil. Serve with the rice.

PER SERVING (1 cup pork mixture with ½ cup rice): 305 Cal, 5 g Fat, 1 g Sat Fat, 0 g Trans Fat, 50 mg Chol, 588 mg Sod, 44 g Carb, 3 g Fib, 23 g Prot, 36 mg Calc. *POINTS* value: *6.*

FOOD NOTE It's a bit more expensive, but consider substituting 1 cup fresh pineapple cubes for the canned—the taste is far superior, and, thanks to prepackaged fresh pineapple now found in the produce section of most supermarkets, it's a breeze.

1 **cup** quick-cooking brown rice

¾ **pound** pork tenderloin, trimmed and thinly sliced

¾ **teaspoon** salt

½ **teaspoon** coarsely ground black pepper

1 **teaspoon** vegetable oil

3 **scallions**, sliced on the diagonal into 2-inch pieces

1 small **apple**, peeled and chopped

1 **red bell pepper**, seeded and chopped

1 **garlic clove**, chopped

¼ **teaspoon** crushed red pepper

1 (8-ounce) can pineapple chunks in juice, drained

½ **cup** Chinese-style sweet-and-sour sauce

Pork Medallions with Ginger Pears and Chutney

PREP	5 MINUTES
COOK	ABOUT 10 MINUTES
SERVES	4

1 Sprinkle the pork with the salt and pepper. Heat 1 teaspoon of the oil in a large nonstick skillet over medium-high heat. Add the pork in a single layer so that the slices don't touch, and cook, in batches if necessary, until browned, about 3 minutes on each side. Transfer the pork to a platter and keep warm.

2 Heat the remaining 1 teaspoon oil in the skillet. Add the pears, ginger, and garlic; cook, stirring frequently, until the pears are tender and golden, about 3 minutes. Add the chutney, broth, and thyme; bring to a boil, stirring to scrape the brown bits from the skillet. Cook until the sauce is slightly thickened, about 2 minutes. Spoon the sauce over the pork.

PER SERVING (2 slices pork with about ½ cup sauce): 201 Cal, 6 g Fat, 1 g Sat Fat, 0 g Trans Fat, 54 mg Chol, 411 mg Sod, 18 g Carb, 2 g Fib, 19 g Prot, 29 mg Calc. **POINTS** value: **4.**

HOW WE DID IT We prefer using ripe but firm Bosc or Anjou pears for the sauce, because both varieties hold up well during cooking.

¾ **pound pork tenderloin**, trimmed and cut into 8 (1-inch-thick) slices

½ **teaspoon salt**

½ **teaspoon coarsely ground black pepper**

2 **teaspoons canola oil**

2 **pears**, peeled and cut into chunks

2 **teaspoons grated peeled fresh ginger**

1 **garlic clove**, minced

¼ **cup mango chutney**

¼ **cup reduced-sodium chicken broth**

2 **teaspoons chopped fresh thyme**, or ½ **teaspoon dried**

Veal Piccata

PREP   5 MINUTES
COOK   ABOUT 10 MINUTES
SERVES 4

1 Cook the rice according to package directions omitting the salt, if desired.

2 Meanwhile, combine the flour, ¼ teaspoon of the salt, and ⅛ teaspoon of the pepper in a shallow bowl. Dip the veal in the flour mixture to coat.

3 Melt 1 tablespoon of the butter in a large nonstick skillet over medium-high heat. Add the veal and cook until browned, 2–3 minutes on each side. Reduce the heat to medium and add the lemon juice, wine, and capers. Cook 1 minute, turning the cutlets once to coat with the wine mixture. Remove the skillet from the heat and transfer the veal to a plate.

4 Add the remaining 1 tablespoon butter, ½ teaspoon salt, and ⅛ teaspoon pepper to the skillet, swirling until the butter melts. Serve the veal and sauce over the rice.

1½ cups quick-cooking white rice

2 tablespoons all-purpose flour

¾ teaspoon salt

¼ teaspoon coarsely ground black pepper

1 pound veal scaloppine

2 tablespoons butter

⅓ cup fresh lemon juice

⅓ cup dry white wine

1 tablespoon capers, drained

PER SERVING (¼ of scaloppine with 2 tablespoons sauce and ½ cup rice): 338 Cal, 8 g Fat, 4 g Sat Fat, 1 g Trans Fat, 105 mg Chol, 648 mg Sod, 36 g Carb, 1 g Fib, 28 g Prot, 12 mg Calc. **POINTS** value: *7.*

FOOD NOTE If you prefer, you can substitute an equal amount of water for the wine in this recipe.

Turkey Rolls Cordon Bleu

PREP 5 MINUTES
COOK ABOUT 10 MINUTES
SERVES 4

1 Top each turkey cutlet with a slice of ham and then a half-slice of cheese. Roll up jelly-roll fashion and secure with toothpicks.

2 Spread the bread crumbs on a plate or a sheet of wax paper. Brush the turkey rolls with the mayonnaise; dip in the crumbs, pressing to coat.

3 Spray a large nonstick skillet with nonstick spray and set over medium-high heat. Add the turkey rolls and cook, stirring occasionally, until browned, about 5 minutes. Add the wine, broth, and butter; bring to a boil. Reduce the heat and simmer, covered, until the turkey rolls are cooked through and the sauce thickens, about 5 minutes.

PER SERVING (1 turkey roll with 2 tablespoons sauce): 146 Cal, 7 g Fat, 3 g Sat Fat, 0 g Trans Fat, 41 mg Chol, 420 mg Sod, 5 g Carb, 0 g Fib, 16 g Prot, 116 mg Calc. **POINTS** value: *4.*

GOOD IDEA If you like your turkey cutlets a bit on the spicy side, brush them with mustard instead of mayonnaise or a combination of the two.

4 (¼-pound) turkey cutlets

4 (1-ounce) slices reduced-sodium ham

2 (1-ounce) slices reduced-fat Swiss cheese, halved

3 tablespoons plain dry bread crumbs

1 tablespoon reduced-calorie mayonnaise

¼ cup dry white wine

¼ cup reduced-sodium chicken broth

1 teaspoon butter

Tortilla Egg Roll-Ups

PREP 5 MINUTES
COOK ABOUT 10 MINUTES
SERVES 4

1 Spray a large nonstick skillet with nonstick spray and set over medium-high heat. Add the bell pepper and cook, stirring frequently, until crisp-tender, about 3 minutes. Add the scallions and tomato; cook, stirring frequently, until softened, about 1 minute. Transfer the vegetables to a plate and set aside.

2 Beat the eggs, egg whites, salt, and pepper sauce in a medium bowl with a fork. Spray the skillet again with nonstick spray. Add the egg mixture and cook, stirring occasionally, until the eggs are scrambled but not dry, about 3 minutes. Remove the pan from the heat and stir in the reserved vegetables.

3 Meanwhile, microwave the tortillas according to package directions. Place the tortillas on a flat surface. Spoon the eggs along the bottom edge of each; sprinkle with the cheese and cilantro. Roll up tightly, then cut in half.

½ green bell pepper, seeded and diced

3 scallions, thinly sliced

1 plum tomato, diced

4 large eggs

4 egg whites

½ teaspoon salt

½ teaspoon hot pepper sauce

4 (6-inch) fat-free flour tortillas

½ cup shredded reduced-fat sharp cheddar cheese

1 tablespoon chopped fresh cilantro

PER SERVING (1 egg roll-up): 201 Cal, 8 g Fat, 3 g Sat Fat, 0 g Trans Fat, 222 mg Chol, 706 mg Sod, 16 g Carb, 7 g Fib, 17 g Prot, 181 mg Calc. **POINTS** value: **4.**

GOOD IDEA Top each roll-up with 2 tablespoons fat-free salsa (the **POINTS** value will remain the same).

**Tortilla Egg
Roll-Ups**

Pierogies with Creamy Mushroom and Sherry Sauce

PREP 5 MINUTES
COOK ABOUT 10 MINUTES
SERVES 4

1 Heat the oil in a large nonstick skillet over medium-high heat. Add the mushrooms, onion, salt, and pepper; cook, stirring occasionally, until tender and lightly browned, about 4 minutes.

2 Stir in the sherry and cook until it evaporates. Sprinkle the flour over the mushroom mixture, stirring to combine. Stir in the milk, broth, and pierogies; bring to a boil. Remove from the heat and stir in the sour cream.

PER SERVING (about 1 ½ cups): 249 Cal, 5 g Fat, 2 g Sat Fat, 0 g Trahhns Fat, 14 mg Chol, 634 mg Sod, 42 g Carb, 3 g Fib, 10 g Prot, 108 mg Calc. **POINTS** value: **5.**

TRY IT *Pierogies* (peer-OH-gees), a Polish specialty, are half-moon-shaped dumplings traditionally made with a variety of fillings, including potato, cabbage, or cheese. Frozen pierogies come in various flavors, any of which would be suitable in this recipe. While most frozen precooked pierogies at the supermarket are relatively low in fat, look for those specifically labeled "low-fat." To thaw frozen pierogies quickly, cook them uncovered in boiling water 3 to 5 minutes, then drain before proceeding with the recipe.

1 teaspoon olive oil

2 cups sliced fresh mushrooms

1 onion, sliced

¼ teaspoon salt

¼ teaspoon coarsely ground black pepper

2 tablespoons dry sherry

1 tablespoon all-purpose flour

⅔ cup low-fat (1%) milk

¼ cup reduced-sodium chicken broth

1 (1-pound) package frozen low-fat potato pierogies, thawed

2 tablespoons light sour cream

Spicy Jack Cheese and Spinach Quesadillas

PREP	5 MINUTES
COOK	ABOUT 10 MINUTES
SERVES	4

1 Mash the avocado, lime juice, and salt in a medium bowl with a fork. Spread a thin layer of the mixture over one-half of each tortilla and divide the spinach among the tortillas. Top each with 1½ teaspoons jalapeño, 1½ teaspoons cilantro, and ¼ cup cheese. Fold the remaining half of each tortilla over the filling.

2 Heat a large nonstick skillet over medium heat. Add 2 quesadillas and cook until the cheese melts and the tortilla browns slightly, about 3 minutes on each side. Transfer to a large serving plate. Repeat with the remaining quesadillas.

PER SERVING (1 quesadilla): 226 Cal, 9 g Fat, 4 g Sat Fat, 0 g Trans Fat, 18 mg Chol, 746 mg Sod, 26 g Carb, 11 g Fib, 14 g Prot, 346 mg Calc. **POINTS** value: **4.**

GOOD IDEA You can change this versatile Southwestern treat to suit your mood. Substitute sautéed sliced mushrooms or rinsed and drained canned beans for the spinach, or add shredded cooked chicken breast (½ cup chicken for each serving will increase the **POINTS** value by 2).

½ cup avocado chunks

1 tablespoon fresh lime juice

¼ teaspoon salt

4 (8-inch) reduced-fat flour tortillas

1 (10-ounce) package frozen chopped spinach, thawed and squeezed dry

2 tablespoons sliced pickled jalapeño, drained

2 tablespoons fresh cilantro leaves

¼ pound reduced-fat Monterey Jack cheese, shredded (about 1 cup)

Tofu Teriyaki

Tofu Teriyaki

PREP 5 MINUTES
COOK ABOUT 10 MINUTES
SERVES 4

1 Cook the rice according to package directions omitting the salt, if desired.

2 Meanwhile, whisk together the soy sauce, vinegar, sugar, cornstarch, and crushed red pepper in a small bowl until smooth; set aside.

3 Heat the oil in a large nonstick skillet over medium-high heat. Add the garlic and cook, stirring frequently, until fragrant, about 30 seconds. Add the vegetables and cook, stirring frequently, until they begin to soften, about 3 minutes. Add the tofu and cook, stirring occasionally, until beginning to brown, about 3 minutes. Stir in the soy sauce mixture and bring to a boil; cook until thickened, about 2 minutes. Serve over the rice.

PER SERVING (1 cup tofu mixture with ½ cup rice): 258 Cal, 6 g Fat, 1 g Sat Fat, 0 g Trans Fat, 0 mg Chol, 557 mg Sod, 35 g Carb, 2 g Fib, 16 g Prot, 224 mg Calc. **POINTS** value: **5.**

GOOD IDEA If your supermarket doesn't carry bags of assorted vegetables precut for stir-fry, create your own mixture from sliced onion, broccoli florets, and bell pepper strips from the salad bar.

1½ cups quick-cooking white rice

¼ cup reduced-sodium soy sauce

2 tablespoons rice vinegar

1 tablespoon sugar

2 teaspoons cornstarch

¼ teaspoon crushed red pepper

1 teaspoon Asian (dark) sesame oil

2 garlic cloves, minced

1 (1-pound) bag fresh precut vegetables for stir-fry

1 pound firm tofu, cut into ½-inch cubes

Just
Chicken

CHAPTER 3

Buffalo Chicken Bites

PREP 10 MINUTES
COOK ABOUT 10 MINUTES
SERVES 4

1 Combine the cayenne pepper sauce, pepper sauce, and Worcestershire sauce in a small saucepan; bring to a boil over medium heat and cook 1 minute. Remove the pan from the heat and stir in 5 teaspoons of the butter until melted.

2 Melt the remaining 1 teaspoon butter in a large nonstick skillet over medium-high heat. Add the chicken and cook, stirring frequently, until well browned and cooked through, 8–10 minutes. Add the pepper sauce mixture and cook about 1 minute, tossing the chicken to coat. Serve with the celery, carrots, and dressing.

PER SERVING (about ½ cup chicken with about 6 celery sticks, 4 carrot sticks, and 2 tablespoons dressing): 246 Cal, 8 g Fat, 4 g Sat Fat, 0 g Trans Fat, 82 mg Chol, 1,340 mg Sod, 16 g Carb, 2 g Fib, 27 g Prot, 36 mg Calc. **POINTS** value: **5.**

EXPRESS LANE Prep twice as many celery and carrot sticks as called for; you'll have extra for a healthy snack another time.

¼ **cup mild cayenne pepper sauce**

1 **teaspoon hot pepper sauce**

1 **teaspoon Worcestershire sauce**

6 **teaspoons butter**

1 **pound skinless boneless chicken breasts, cut into 1-inch chunks**

3 **celery stalks, cut into sticks**

2 **carrots, cut into sticks**

½ **cup fat-free blue cheese dressing**

Chicken Cheddar Hoagies

PREP   10 MINUTES
COOK   ABOUT 10 MINUTES
SERVES   4

1 Heat 1 teaspoon of the oil in a large nonstick skillet over medium-high heat. Add the onion, bell peppers, and thyme; cook, stirring occasionally, until softened, 4–5 minutes. Add the Worcestershire sauce, ¼ teaspoon of the salt, and ⅛ teaspoon of the ground pepper; cook until the flavors are blended, about 2 minutes. Transfer the onion mixture to a bowl.

2 Sprinkle the chicken with the remaining ¼ teaspoon salt and ⅛ teaspoon ground pepper. Heat the remaining 1 teaspoon oil in the skillet. Add the chicken and cook until lightly browned, about 3 minutes. Turn the chicken over and top each piece with ¼ cup of the onion mixture and 2 tablespoons of the cheese. Cover and cook until the chicken is cooked through and the cheese melts, about 2 minutes.

3 Mound ¼ cup of the remaining onion mixture on each of the sandwich bottoms and top with the chicken; cover with the tops.

PER SERVING (1 sandwich): 387 Cal, 9 g Fat, 3 g Sat Fat, 0 g Trans Fat, 80 mg Chol, 814 mg Sod, 38 g Carb, 4 g Fib, 37 g Prot, 205 mg Calc. **POINTS** value: **8.**

2 teaspoons olive oil

1 large onion, sliced

1 red bell pepper, seeded and sliced

1 green bell pepper, seeded and sliced

½ teaspoon dried thyme

1 tablespoon Worcestershire sauce

½ teaspoon salt

¼ teaspoon coarsely ground black pepper

4 (¼-pound) thin-sliced chicken breast cutlets

½ cup shredded reduced-fat sharp cheddar cheese

½ pound Italian bread (about ½ loaf), partially split open and cut crosswise into 4 pieces

California Chicken Salad

California Chicken Salad

PREP 20 MINUTES
COOK ABOUT 10 MINUTES
SERVES 4

1 Bring the broth to a boil in a large skillet over medium-high heat. Add the chicken, reduce the heat, and simmer until cooked through, about 10 minutes. Remove the chicken from the broth and let cool 2 minutes. Cut the chicken into thin slices and arrange in a row across the center of a platter. Discard the broth.

2 Arrange the grapes, tomato, apple, orange, avocado, and red onion in rows alongside the chicken. Combine the orange juice, mustard, salt, and pepper in a small bowl. Drizzle the dressing over the salad.

PER SERVING (1½ cups): 263 Cal, 7 g Fat, 2 g Sat Fat, 0 g Trans Fat, 72 mg Chol, 409 mg Sod, 22 g Carb, 4 g Fib, 28 g Prot, 45 mg Calc. *POINTS* value: *5.*

HOW WE DID IT To peel and section an orange, cut off the ends with a sharp knife. Place the orange cut-end down and slice off the peel as close to flesh as possible from top to bottom. (Make sure to remove all the bitter white portion or pith.) Holding the orange over a bowl to save any juice, use a small paring knife to slice between the membrane. Gently lift out the orange sections. Continue working all the way around the orange.

1¾ cups reduced-sodium chicken broth

1 pound skinless boneless chicken breasts

1 cup seedless green grapes, halved

1 tomato, cut into thin wedges

1 Granny Smith apple, cut into thin slices

1 orange, peeled and cut into sections

1 cup thinly sliced avocado (preferably Haas)

⅓ cup thinly sliced red onion

¼ cup orange juice

2 teaspoons Dijon mustard

½ teaspoon salt

⅛ teaspoon coarsely ground black pepper

Polynesian Pineapple Chicken

PREP 15 MINUTES
COOK ABOUT 15 MINUTES
SERVES 4

1 Whisk together the ketchup, soy sauce, sugar, vinegar, and cornstarch in a bowl until smooth; set aside.

2 Heat 2 teaspoons of the oil in a large nonstick skillet over medium-high heat. Add the chicken and cook, stirring occasionally, until cooked through, 5–6 minutes. Transfer the chicken to a plate.

3 Heat the remaining 1 teaspoon oil in the skillet. Add the carrots and ginger; cook, stirring occasionally, until the carrots begin to soften, about 2 minutes. Stir in the snow peas, almonds, water chestnuts, pineapple, and the chicken. Cook, stirring frequently, until the snow peas are crisp-tender, 3–4 minutes. Add the ketchup mixture; bring to a boil and cook, stirring constantly, until thickened, about 1 minute.

PER SERVING (about 1¾ cups): 363 Cal, 10 g Fat, 1 g Sat Fat, 0 g Trans Fat, 66 mg Chol, 760 mg Sod, 37 g Carb, 6 g Fib, 32 g Prot, 79 mg Calc. *POINTS* value: *7.*

GOOD IDEA This chicken dish goes well over quick-cooking brown rice (½ cup cooked rice for each serving will increase the *POINTS* value by 2). Because brown rice has a high-fiber bran coating, it goes rancid quickly and should only be stored for 6 months on the pantry shelf. It will last much longer kept in the refrigerator.

- ⅓ cup ketchup
- 3 tablespoons reduced-sodium soy sauce
- 3 tablespoons sugar
- 2 tablespoons rice vinegar
- 1 tablespoon cornstarch
- 3 teaspoons canola oil
- 1 pound skinless boneless chicken breasts, cut into ½-inch cubes
- 2 carrots, thinly sliced
- 1 tablespoon minced peeled fresh ginger
- ½ pound fresh snow peas, trimmed
- ¼ cup sliced almonds
- 1 (8-ounce) can water chestnuts, drained
- 1 (8-ounce) can pineapple chunks in juice, drained

Polynesian Pineapple Chicken

Greek Chicken Pasta Toss

PREP 10 MINUTES
COOK ABOUT 20 MINUTES
SERVES 6

1 Cook the rotini according to package directions omitting the salt, if desired; drain.

2 Meanwhile, sprinkle the chicken with the salt and ground pepper. Heat 1 tablespoon of the oil in a large nonstick skillet over medium-high heat. Add the chicken and cook, stirring occasionally, until lightly browned and cooked through, 6–7 minutes. Transfer the chicken to a plate.

3 Heat the remaining 1 tablespoon oil in the skillet. Add the garlic and oregano; cook, stirring constantly, until the garlic is fragrant, about 30 seconds. Add the roasted peppers, artichoke hearts, and tomatoes; cook until the tomatoes begin to soften, about 3 minutes. Add the lemon juice and the chicken; cook until heated through, about 1 minute. Transfer to a large bowl and add the rotini, feta, and Parmesan. Toss well. Serve warm or at room temperature.

PER SERVING (about 1 cup): 334 Cal, 9 g Fat, 3 g Sat Fat, 0 g Trans Fat, 53 mg Chol, 500 mg Sod, 37 g Carb, 2 g Fib, 26 g Prot, 96 mg Calc. *POINTS* value: *7.*

EXPRESS LANE To trim the prep time, start with presliced chicken tenders.

½ **pound rotini**

1 **pound skinless boneless chicken breasts,** cut into thin strips

¼ **teaspoon salt**

¼ **teaspoon coarsely ground black pepper**

2 **tablespoons extra-virgin olive oil**

3 **garlic cloves, thinly sliced**

1 **teaspoon dried oregano**

1 (7-ounce) jar **roasted red peppers,** drained and thinly sliced

1 (14-ounce) can **artichoke hearts,** drained and quartered

1 pint **cherry tomatoes,** halved

2 tablespoons **fresh lemon juice**

2 ounces **feta cheese,** crumbled

2 tablespoons grated **Parmesan cheese**

Chicken-Spinach Stir-Fry

PREP 10 MINUTES PLUS 1 HOUR MARINATING TIME
COOK ABOUT 5 MINUTES
SERVES 2

1 Combine the soy sauce, cornstarch, wine, honey, ginger, and nutmeg in a zip-close plastic bag; add the chicken. Squeeze out the air and seal the bag; turn to coat the chicken. Refrigerate, turning the bag occasionally, 1 hour.

2 Heat a large nonstick skillet or wok over high heat until a drop of water sizzles. Add the oil, swirl to coat the pan, then add the chicken and marinade. Stir-fry until the chicken is lightly colored and cooked through and the marinade is boiling, about 3 minutes. Add the celery and stir-fry until crisp-tender, about 1 minute. Stir in the spinach and stir-fry until the spinach is wilted and the celery is softened, 2–3 minutes.

PER SERVING (1 cup): 153 Cal, 4 g Fat, 1 g Sat Fat, 0 g Trans Fat, 41 mg Chol, 448 mg Sod, 10 g Carb, 3 g Fib, 20 g Prot, 127 mg Calc. **POINTS** value: **3.**

GOOD IDEA Skip cleaning and tearing the spinach leaves by using packaged baby spinach.

1 tablespoon reduced-sodium soy sauce

2 teaspoons cornstarch

2 teaspoons rice wine or dry sherry

½ teaspoon honey

¼ teaspoon ground ginger

⅛ teaspoon ground nutmeg

¼ pound skinless boneless chicken breast, cut into strips

1 teaspoon peanut oil

1 celery stalk, thinly sliced

4 cups torn cleaned spinach

Chicken Marsala

Chicken Marsala

PREP   10 MINUTES
COOK   ABOUT 10 MINUTES
SERVES 4

1 Sprinkle the chicken with the salt and pepper.

2 Heat the oil in a large nonstick skillet over medium-high heat. Add the chicken and cook until cooked through, about 3 minutes on each side. Transfer the chicken to a platter and keep warm.

3 Add the mushrooms to the skillet and cook, stirring frequently, until browned, about 3 minutes. Sprinkle the mushrooms with the flour, stirring to blend. Add the Marsala and broth; bring to a boil. Cook, stirring occasionally, until the sauce thickens, about 3 minutes. Spoon the sauce over the chicken.

PER SERVING (1 chicken cutlet with ¼ cup sauce): 164 Cal, 4 g Fat, 1 g Sat Fat, 0 g Trans Fat, 66 mg Chol, 430 mg Sod, 3 g Carb, 0 g Fib, 28 g Prot, 17 mg Calc. **POINTS** value: **4.**

GOOD IDEA If you like, try shiitake or Portobello mushrooms in the sauce for a more intense mushroom flavor.

4 (¼-pound) thin-sliced chicken breast cutlets

½ teaspoon salt

½ teaspoon coarsely ground black pepper

2 teaspoons olive oil

2 cups sliced fresh mushrooms

2 teaspoons all-purpose flour

¼ cup Marsala

¼ cup reduced-sodium chicken broth

Shiitake-Chicken Stir-Fry

PREP 10 MINUTES PLUS 10 MINUTES STANDING TIME
COOK ABOUT 10 MINUTES
SERVES 4

1 Place the noodles in a large bowl with enough hot water to cover. Let stand until softened, about 10 minutes. Drain and transfer to a serving platter; keep warm.

2 Meanwhile, heat a large nonstick skillet or wok over high heat until a drop of water sizzles. Add the oil, swirl to coat the pan, then add the garlic and ginger. Stir-fry until just fragrant, about 15 seconds. Add the bell peppers, broccoli, mushrooms, and scallions; stir-fry until the vegetables are just tender, about 3 minutes. Transfer the vegetables to a plate.

3 Add the chicken to the skillet and stir-fry, adding the broth as needed to prevent sticking, until lightly browned and cooked through, about 4 minutes. Add the vegetables and soy sauce; stir-fry until the vegetables are heated through, about 2 minutes. Serve over the noodles; sprinkle with the salt and ground pepper.

PER SERVING (2 cups): 316 Cal, 6 g Fat, 1 g Sat Fat, 0 g Trans Fat, 52 mg Chol, 484 mg Sod, 44 g Carb, 3 g Fib, 22 g Prot, 51 mg Calc. **POINTS** value: **6.**

TRY IT *Shiitake* (shee-TAH-kay) mushrooms have meaty-textured dark brown caps and tough, almost inedible stems. Always separate the two before cooking, but don't discard the stems. Toss them into soups and sauces, where they'll release their magnificent, smoky flavor; remove them before serving (as you would a bay leaf).

6 ounces cellophane noodles

1 tablespoon peanut oil

3 garlic cloves, minced

1 (½-inch) piece peeled fresh ginger, sliced

½ yellow bell pepper, seeded and sliced

½ orange bell pepper, seeded and sliced

1 cup fresh broccoli florets

1 cup sliced fresh shiitake mushrooms

8 scallions, thinly sliced

¾ pound skinless boneless chicken breasts, cut into strips

1–2 tablespoons chicken broth or water

1 tablespoon reduced-sodium soy sauce

½ teaspoon salt

¼ teaspoon freshly ground pepper

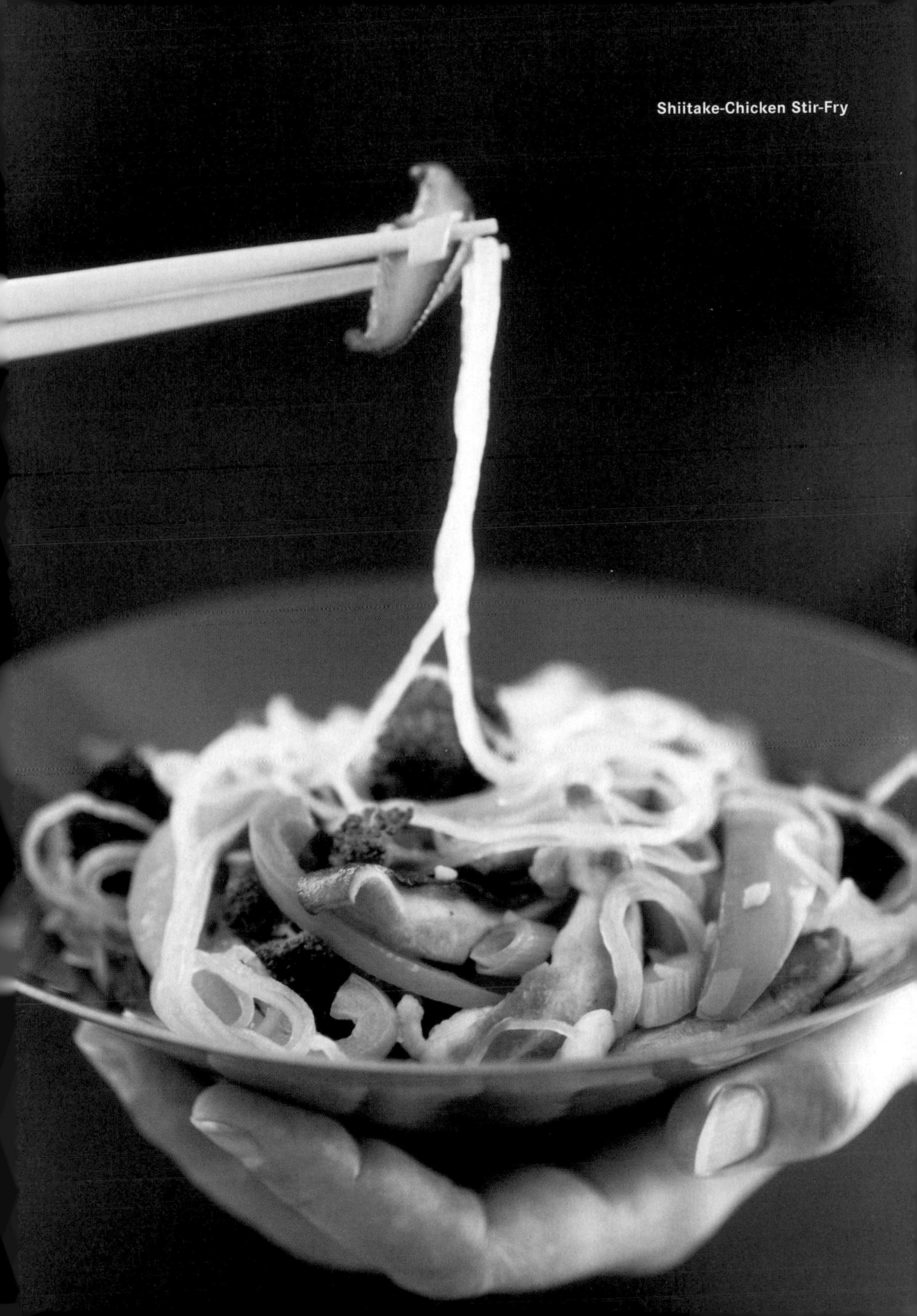

Shiitake-Chicken Stir-Fry

Zesty Chicken with Shallots, Capers, and Olives

PREP 10 MINUTES
COOK ABOUT 20 MINUTES
SERVES 4

1 Sprinkle both sides of the chicken with the rosemary, salt, and pepper.

2 Heat the oil in a large nonstick skillet over medium-high heat. Add the chicken and cook until browned and cooked through, about 3 minutes on each side. Transfer the chicken to a plate.

3 Add the shallots and garlic to the skillet; cook until the shallots are softened, about 1 minute. Stir in the vinegar and cook until it evaporates, about 30 seconds. Add the tomatoes, wine, olives, and capers; bring to a boil. Reduce the heat and simmer until the sauce thickens slightly, about 8 minutes. Stir in the basil. Return the chicken to the skillet and cook until heated through, about 1 minute.

PER SERVING (about 1 cup): 186 Cal, 4 g Fat, 1 g Sat Fat, 0 g Trans Fat, 66 mg Chol, 878 mg Sod, 8 g Carb, 1 g Fib, 28 g Prot, 34 mg Calc. *POINTS* value: *4.*

GOOD IDEA Serve this dish over your favorite thin-strand pasta with a tossed green salad on the side (½ cup cooked pasta for each serving will increase the *POINTS* value by 2).

1 pound thin-sliced chicken breast cutlets

1 teaspoon dried rosemary, crumbled

½ teaspoon salt

½ teaspoon coarsely ground black pepper

2 teaspoons olive oil

2 shallots, chopped

1 garlic clove, minced

3 tablespoons apple-cider vinegar

1 (14½-ounce) can diced tomatoes, with their juice

¼ cup dry white wine

5 kalamata olives, pitted and chopped

1 tablespoon capers, drained

¼ cup chopped fresh basil

Cider Chicken with Apples and Thyme

PREP 10 MINUTES
COOK ABOUT 30 MINUTES
SERVES 4

1 Sprinkle the chicken with the salt and pepper.

2 Heat the oil in a large nonstick skillet over medium-high heat. Add the chicken and cook until golden and cooked through, about 4 minutes on each side. Transfer the chicken to a plate.

3 Add the onions and bacon to the skillet. Cook, shaking the pan occasionally, until the onions are softened and browned, about 8 minutes. Add the apple and thyme; cook until the apple is tender and golden, about 5 minutes. Stir in the cider and broth. Increase the heat and cook until the sauce boils and thickens slightly, about 5 minutes. Return the chicken to the skillet and cook until heated through, about 2 minutes. Garnish with the thyme sprigs.

PER SERVING (1 chicken breast with ½ cup sauce): 270 Cal, 7 g Fat, 1 g Sat Fat, 0 g Trans Fat, 92 mg Chol, 617 mg Sod, 16 g Carb, 2 g Fib, 35 g Prot, 67 mg Calc. **POINTS** value: **6.**

GOOD IDEA Choose a firm apple that will hold its shape while cooking; we call for Golden Delicious, but a Granny Smith would work well, too.

4 (5-ounce) skinless boneless chicken breasts

½ teaspoon salt

½ teaspoon coarsely ground black pepper

2 teaspoons olive oil

1 cup frozen pearl onions, thawed

4 strips turkey bacon, diced

1 Golden Delicious apple, cut into chunks

1 tablespoon chopped fresh thyme, or 1 teaspoon dried

1 cup apple cider

¼ cup reduced-sodium chicken broth

Fresh thyme sprigs, for garnish

Chicken Calvados

Chicken Calvados

PREP 20 MINUTES
COOK ABOUT 25 MINUTES
SERVES 4

1 Combine the salt, pepper, cinnamon, and ginger in a small bowl. Rub the mixture over both sides of each chicken breast.

2 Heat the oil in a large nonstick skillet over medium-high heat. Add the chicken and cook until browned, about 3 minutes on each side. Transfer to a plate.

3 Add the onions to the skillet and cook, stirring occasionally, until softened, about 5 minutes. Add the apples and cook, stirring occasionally, until golden brown and tender, 3–5 minutes. Stir in the cider; bring to a boil. Return the chicken to the skillet and cook, turning occasionally, until cooked through, about 5 minutes. Transfer to a platter.

4 Stir the Calvados into the skillet and cook until the apples and onions are glazed and the liquid is thickened, about 3 minutes. Serve the chicken topped with the apple mixture.

PER SERVING (1 chicken breast with ¾ cup apple mixture): 286 Cal, 6 g Fat, 1 g Sat Fat, 0 g Trans Fat, 66 mg Chol, 350 mg Sod, 28 g Carb, 3 g Fib, 27 g Prot, 33 mg Calc. *POINTS* value: *6.*

½ teaspoon salt

½ teaspoon freshly ground pepper

¼ teaspoon cinnamon

¼ teaspoon ground ginger

4 (¼-pound) skinless boneless chicken breasts

4 teaspoons vegetable oil

2 onions, thinly sliced

4 Golden Delicious apples, peeled and thinly sliced

1 cup apple cider or apple juice

2 tablespoons Calvados (apple brandy)

TRY IT *Calvados* (KAL-vah-dohs), a French apple brandy produced in Normandy, is distilled from cider, in much the same way that cognac and Armagnac are distilled from wine. Its flavor marries well with pork dishes. If you prefer, use apple jack or plain brandy.

Lemon Chicken

PREP 10 MINUTES
COOK ABOUT 10 MINUTES
SERVES 4

1 On a sheet of wax paper, combine the flour, salt, and pepper. Coat one side of each chicken cutlet with the flour mixture.

2 Heat the oil in a large nonstick skillet over medium-high heat. Add the chicken, floured-side down, and cook until lightly browned and cooked through, about 1 minute on each side. Transfer to a plate.

3 Add the broth, lemon juice, parsley, and capers to the skillet; bring to a boil. Cook until the liquid is reduced to about ⅓ cup, about 2 minutes. Return the chicken and any accumulated juices to the skillet; cook until just heated through, about 2 minutes. Serve, garnished with the lemon slices.

PER SERVING (1 chicken breast with 2 tablespoons sauce): 167 Cal, 5 g Fat, 1 g Sat Fat, 0 g Trans Fat, 71 mg Chol, 365 mg Sod, 2 g Carb, 0 g Fib, 26 g Prot, 16 mg Calc. **POINTS** value: **4.**

GOOD IDEA If you're following the **Core Plan**, just sprinkle the chicken with the salt and pepper and skip the flour in step 1.

1 **tablespoon
all-purpose flour**

¼ **teaspoon** salt

¼ **teaspoon freshly
ground pepper**

4 **(¼-pound) thin-sliced
chicken breast cutlets**

2 **teaspoons** olive oil

½ **cup chicken broth**

2 **tablespoons fresh
lemon juice**

1 **tablespoon chopped
fresh flat-leaf parsley**

1 **tablespoon** capers,
rinsed and drained

**Lemon slices, for
garnish**

Easy Skillet Chicken

PREP 15 MINUTES
COOK ABOUT 25 MINUTES
SERVES 4

1 Heat the oil in a large nonstick skillet over medium-high heat. Add the onions, carrot, and celery; cook, stirring occasionally, until softened, about 10 minutes. Add the chicken and cook, stirring frequently, until cooked through, about 5 minutes.

2 Stir in the tomatoes, cheese, basil, salt, and pepper. Reduce the heat and simmer, stirring occasionally, until the flavors are blended, about 10 minutes.

PER SERVING (1 cup): 175 Cal, 6 g Fat, 1 g Sat Fat, 0 g Trans Fat, 53 mg Chol, 385 mg Sod, 8 g Carb, 2 g Fib, 21 g Prot, 62 mg Calc. **POINTS** value: *4.*

PLAY IT SAFE To keep chicken fresh, it should be refrigerated (it's fine to leave it in its original wrapper) in the coldest part of the refrigerator (usually the bottom shelf in the back) up to 2 days from purchase.

1 tablespoon olive oil

2 onions, chopped

1 carrot, chopped

1 celery stalk, sliced

¾ pound skinless boneless chicken breasts, cut into thin strips

1 (14½-ounce) can crushed tomatoes

4 teaspoons grated Parmesan cheese

1 tablespoon chopped fresh basil

½ teaspoon salt

¼ teaspoon freshly ground pepper

Skillet Yellow Rice and Chicken

PREP   15 MINUTES
COOK   ABOUT 30 MINUTES
SERVES   4

1 Heat the oil in a large nonstick skillet over medium-high heat. Add the onion, bell pepper, and garlic; cook, stirring frequently, until softened, about 2 minutes. Add the chicken and cook, stirring frequently, until lightly browned, about 2 minutes.

2 Stir in the rice, turmeric, and cumin; cook, stirring constantly, until the rice is well coated, about 1 minute. Add the broth, olives, capers, salt, and ground pepper; bring to a boil. Reduce the heat and simmer, covered, until the rice is tender and the liquid evaporates, about 15 minutes. Remove the skillet from the heat and stir in the parsley.

PER SERVING (1 cup): 375 Cal, 9 g Fat, 2 g Sat Fat, 0 g Trans Fat, 94 mg Chol, 943 mg Sod, 42 g Carb, 2 g Fib, 28 g Prot, 61 mg Calc. **POINTS** value: **8.**

EXPRESS LANE To shave a few minutes more off the prep time, use ¼ cup presliced Spanish olives, instead of slicing whole olives yourself.

- 1 tablespoon olive oil
- ½ cup chopped onion
- ½ cup chopped green bell pepper
- 2 garlic cloves, minced
- 1 pound skinless boneless chicken thighs, cut into 1-inch pieces
- 1 cup long-grain white rice
- 1 teaspoon turmeric
- 1 teaspoon ground cumin
- 2 cups reduced-sodium chicken broth
- 10 pimiento-stuffed green olives, halved crosswise
- 1 tablespoon capers, drained
- ½ teaspoon salt
- ½ teaspoon coarsely ground black pepper
- ¼ cup chopped fresh parsley

Almond Chicken and Asparagus

PREP 20 MINUTES
COOK ABOUT 30 MINUTES
SERVES 4

1 Whisk together the egg white, wine, cornstarch, sugar, salt, and five-spice powder in a small bowl until smooth. Dip each chicken strip into the mixture to coat, then into the almonds to coat.

2 Heat a large nonstick skillet or wok over high heat until a drop of water sizzles. Add the oil, swirl to coat the pan, then add half the chicken strips. Stir-fry until the edges are golden and the chicken is cooked through, 2–3 minutes. Place the chicken in a mound on top of the asparagus; keep warm. Repeat with remaining chicken. Sprinkle with the cilantro; serve at once, or refrigerate up to 2 days.

PER SERVING (¾ cup chicken with 1 cup asparagus): 202 Cal, 10 g Fat, 1 g Sat Fat, 0 g Trans Fat, 33 mg Chol, 88 mg Sod, 10 g Carb, 3 g Fib, 21 g Prot, 73 mg Calc. **POINTS** value: **4.**

HOW WE DID IT To toast the almonds, preheat the oven to 350°F. Spread the almonds in a shallow baking pan; bake, stirring as needed, until golden brown, 10 to 15 minutes.

1 **egg white**

1 **tablespoon** rice wine or dry sherry

2 **teaspoons** cornstarch

1 **teaspoon** sugar

Pinch salt

Pinch five-spice powder

½ **pound** skinless boneless chicken breasts, **cut into thin strips**

½ **cup** almonds, **toasted and finely chopped**

1 **teaspoon** peanut oil

36 **fresh asparagus spears, trimmed, cut into 2-inch pieces, and steamed**

1 **tablespoon minced fresh cilantro**

Chicken Fried Rice

PREP 10 MINUTES
COOK ABOUT 15 MINUTES
SERVES 6

1 Heat a large nonstick skillet or wok over high heat until a drop of water sizzles. Add 2 teaspoons of the canola oil, swirl to coat the pan, then add the eggs. Stir-fry until firmly scrambled, about 2 minutes. Transfer the eggs to a bowl.

2 Add 1 teaspoon of the canola oil to the skillet, swirl to coat the pan, then add the chicken. Stir-fry until cooked through, 6–7 minutes; transfer to the bowl with the eggs.

3 Meanwhile, place the rice in a shallow bowl. With moistened fingers, stir the rice to separate the grains.

4 Add the remaining 1 tablespoon canola oil to the skillet, swirl to coat the pan, then add the scallions, ginger, and garlic. Stir-fry until fragrant, about 1 minute. Add the rice and peas and carrots; stir-fry about 2 minutes. Stir in the eggs and chicken, the soy sauce, and sesame oil; cook, stirring frequently, until heated through, about 5 minutes.

PER SERVING (1 cup): 325 Cal, 8 g Fat, 1 g Sat Fat, 0 g Trans Fat, 115 mg Chol, 373 mg Sod, 36 g Carb, 2 g Fib, 25 g Prot, 41 mg Calc. *POINTS* value: *7.*

3 teaspoons + 1 tablespoon canola oil

2 large eggs, beaten

1 pound skinless boneless chicken breasts, cut into thin strips

4 cups cold cooked long-grain white rice

1 cup chopped scallions (8–10 scallions)

1 tablespoon minced peeled fresh ginger

1 garlic clove, minced

1½ cups frozen peas and carrots

3 tablespoons reduced-sodium soy sauce

1 teaspoon Asian (dark) sesame oil

GOOD IDEA Fried rice works best when you start with cold, day-old rice, which is drier than freshly cooked rice. To make the rice ahead, spread the hot rice on a baking sheet to cool quickly before you refrigerate. Or, freeze leftover cooked rice to have on hand when the urge for a quick Chinese meal strikes.

Chicken Ragoût with
Potatoes and Olives

Chicken Ragoût with Potatoes and Olives

PREP   15 MINUTES
COOK   ABOUT 30 MINUTES
SERVES 4

1 Sprinkle the chicken with the salt and pepper.

2 Heat the oil in a large nonstick skillet over medium-high heat. Add the chicken and cook until browned, 2–3 minutes on each side. Add the onion and garlic; cook until the onion is just tender, about 5 minutes. Stir in the tomatoes, potato, olives, broth, and wine; bring to a boil. Reduce the heat and simmer, covered, until the chicken is cooked through and the potato is tender, about 20 minutes. Remove the skillet from the heat and stir in the basil.

PER SERVING (1½ cups): 306 Cal, 9 g Fat, 2 g Sat Fat, 0 g Trans Fat, 141 mg Chol, 600 mg Sod, 19 g Carb, 3 g Fib, 36 g Prot, 52 mg Calc. **POINTS** value: *6.*

GOOD IDEA Vary the herb to suit your fancy; just be sure to stir it in at the very end of cooking to maximize fresh flavor. To store fresh basil or other herbs, place the stem ends in a glass or jar of cold water; cover the top of the bunch with a plastic food-storage bag, and refrigerate.

1½ **pounds** skinless boneless chicken thighs

½ **teaspoon** salt

¼ **teaspoon coarsely ground black pepper**

1 **teaspoon** olive oil

1 **onion, thinly sliced**

1 **garlic clove, chopped**

3 **plum tomatoes, chopped**

1 **large baking potato, peeled and cubed**

10 **kalamata olives, pitted and sliced**

½ **cup reduced-sodium chicken broth**

¼ **cup** dry white wine

½ **cup chopped fresh basil**

Pasta and Noodles

CHAPTER 4

Orange Beef with Noodles

PREP 10 MINUTES PLUS 20 MINUTES STANDING TIME
COOK ABOUT 10 MINUTES
SERVES 4

1 Place the noodles in a large bowl with enough hot water to cover. Let stand until softened, about 20 minutes; drain.

2 Meanwhile, whisk together the orange juice, soy sauce, sugar, sesame oil, cornstarch, and chili paste in a bowl until smooth; set aside.

3 Spray a large nonstick skillet with nonstick spray and set over medium-high heat. Add the steak and stir-fry in batches, until browned, about 5 minutes. Add the scallions, garlic, and ginger. Stir-fry until fragrant, about 3 minutes. Stir in the orange juice mixture and cook until the sauce boils and is slightly thickened, about 3 minutes. Stir in the noodles; heat through.

PER SERVING (1 ¼ cups): 210 Cal, 5 g Fat, 2 g Sat Fat, 1 g Trans Fat, 32 mg Chol, 342 mg Sod, 26 g Carb, 1 g Fib, 14 g Prot, 34 mg Calc. *POINTS* value: *4.*

TRY IT Rice stick noodles—long, thin translucent noodles made of rice flour—are commonly used in Thai cooking. Look for them in Asian markets or larger supermarkets.

- ¼ **pound** rice stick noodles
- ⅔ **cup** orange juice
- 2 **tablespoons** reduced-sodium soy sauce
- 2 **teaspoons** sugar
- 1 **teaspoon** Asian (dark) sesame oil
- 1 **teaspoon** cornstarch
- ½ **teaspoon** hot chili paste
- ½ **pound** flank steak, trimmed and cut into thin strips
- 6 scallions, cut into 2-inch pieces
- 2 garlic cloves, minced
- 2 teaspoons chopped peeled fresh ginger

Orange Beef with Noodles

Spaghetti Bolognese

PREP 15 MINUTES
COOK ABOUT 40 MINUTES
SERVES 4

1 Heat a large nonstick skillet over medium-high heat. Add the beef and cook, breaking it up with a wooden spoon, until browned, 5–6 minutes. Add the onion and garlic; cook, stirring occasionally, until softened, about 5 minutes. Add the carrot and cook, stirring occasionally, until crisp-tender, about 2 minutes. Stir in the mushrooms, tomatoes, tomato paste, basil, oregano, and parsley; bring to a boil. Reduce the heat and simmer, covered, about 10 minutes; add the milk and cook, uncovered, until the sauce is thickened, about 15 minutes. Stir in the salt and pepper.

2 Meanwhile, cook the spaghetti according to package directions omitting the salt, if desired; drain. Divide the spaghetti among 4 plates and top with the sauce. Serve, sprinkled with the cheese.

PER SERVING (about 2 cups): 386 Cal, 8 g Fat, 3 g Sat Fat, 1 g Trans Fat, 25 mg Chol, 736 mg Sod, 56 g Carb, 6 g Fib, 24 g Prot, 99 mg Calc. *POINTS* value: *8.*

EXPRESS LANE This meaty sauce freezes beautifully—so grab another skillet and make a double batch, then thaw half for an almost instant supper on a busy weeknight.

¾ pound ground lean beef (7% or less fat)

1 onion, finely chopped

2 garlic cloves, minced

1 carrot, chopped

3 cups sliced fresh mushrooms

1 (14½-ounce) can Italian stewed tomatoes

1 tablespoon tomato paste

½ teaspoon dried basil

½ teaspoon dried oregano

½ teaspoon dried parsley

¼ cup low-fat (1%) milk

½ teaspoon salt

¼ teaspoon freshly ground pepper

½ pound spaghetti

4 teaspoons grated Parmesan cheese

Cellophane Noodles with Pork

PREP 10 MINUTES PLUS 30 MINUTES MARINATING AND STANDING TIME
COOK ABOUT 10 MINUTES
SERVES 4

1 Combine the pork, soy sauce, ketchup, hoisin sauce, vinegar, and garlic in a medium bowl; mix well. Cover and refrigerate until the flavors are blended, about 20 minutes.

2 Meanwhile, place the noodles in a medium bowl with enough hot water to cover. Let stand until softened, about 10 minutes; drain.

3 Heat a large nonstick skillet or wok over high heat until a drop of water sizzles. Add 1 teaspoon of the oil, swirl to coat the pan, then add the pork mixture. Stir-fry, breaking it up with a wooden spoon, until cooked through, about 4 minutes. Transfer the pork and pan juices to a plate and keep warm.

4 Add the remaining 1 teaspoon oil to the skillet, swirl to coat the pan, then add the scallions and ginger. Stir-fry until just fragrant, about 15 seconds. Add the chili paste and stir-fry about 5 seconds. Add the pork, noodles, and broth; bring to a boil. Reduce the heat and simmer, stirring gently, until the noodles have absorbed most of the liquid, 3–4 minutes. Sprinkle with the cilantro.

PER SERVING (about 1 cup): 173 Cal, 6 g Fat, 2 g Sat Fat, 0 g Trans Fat, 23 mg Chol, 337 mg Sod, 22 g Carb, 1 g Fib, 8 g Prot, 23 mg Calc. ***POINTS*** value: *4.*

- 5 **ounces** ground lean pork
- 1 **tablespoon** reduced-sodium soy sauce
- 1 **tablespoon** ketchup
- 2 **teaspoons** hoisin sauce
- 1 **teaspoon** rice vinegar
- 2 **garlic cloves**, minced
- ¼ **pound** cellophane noodles
- 2 **teaspoons** peanut oil
- 2 **scallions**, minced
- ½ **teaspoon** minced peeled fresh ginger
- 1 **teaspoon** hot chili paste
- 1 **cup** reduced-sodium chicken broth
- 1 **tablespoon** minced fresh cilantro

HOW WE DID IT For truly lean ground pork, start with a well-trimmed lean cut like loin and grind it in your food processor.

Pan-Fried Noodles with Spicy Lamb

PREP   15 MINUTES PLUS ABOUT 1 HOUR MARINATING AND COOLING TIME
COOK   ABOUT 40 MINUTES
SERVES   4

1 Combine the broth, wine, soy sauce, vinegar, 1 teaspoon of the sesame oil, the sugar, and crushed red pepper in a zip-close plastic bag; add the lamb. Seal the bag; turn to coat the lamb. Refrigerate 1 hour. Drain the lamb, reserving the marinade.

2 Meanwhile, cook the noodles according to package directions omitting the salt, if desired; drain. Transfer the noodles to a plate. Add the remaining ½ teaspoon sesame oil and toss lightly; let cool.

3 Whisk together the reserved marinade, the water, and cornstarch in a small bowl until smooth; set aside.

4 Heat a large nonstick skillet or wok over high heat until a drop of water sizzles. Add ½ teaspoon of the peanut oil, swirl to coat the pan, then add the noodles. Cook, turning with a spatula until lightly browned, about 4 minutes. Transfer to a serving platter and keep warm.

5 Add 1 teaspoon of the peanut oil to the skillet, swirl to coat the pan, then add the lamb. Stir-fry until barely pink, 2–3 minutes; transfer to a plate and keep warm.

6 Add the remaining 1 teaspoon peanut oil to the skillet, swirl to coat the pan, then add the scallions, garlic, and ginger. Stir-fry until the scallions are softened, 2–3 minutes. Add the bell peppers and stir-fry until softened, about 5 minutes. Add the lamb and the marinade mixture; bring to a rolling boil and cook until the sauce thickens and coats the lamb, about 1 minute. Pour the mixture over the noodles; serve at once.

Per serving (about 1 ½ cups): 276 Cal, 10 g Fat, 2 g Sat Fat, 0 g Trans Fat, 68 mg Chol, 204 mg Sod, 29 g Carb, 2 g Fib, 16 g Prot, 35 mg Calc. **POINTS** value: **6.**

2 **tablespoons reduced-sodium chicken broth**

1 **tablespoon rice wine or dry sherry**

1 **tablespoon reduced-sodium soy sauce**

2 **teaspoons rice vinegar**

1½ **teaspoons Asian (dark) sesame oil**

½ **teaspoon sugar**

Pinch crushed red pepper

½ **pound boneless lamb shoulder or leg, trimmed and cut into thin strips**

¼ **pound thin egg noodle clusters or fideos**

2 **tablespoons water**

1 **tablespoon cornstarch**

2½ **teaspoons peanut oil**

8 **scallions, thinly sliced**

1 **garlic clove, minced**

1 **(½-inch) piece peeled fresh ginger, minced**

1 **green bell pepper, seeded and cut into strips**

½ **red bell pepper, seeded and cut into strips**

**Pan-Fried Noodles
with Spicy Lamb**

Noodle Cake with Lamb

PREP   20 MINUTES PLUS ABOUT 2 HOURS MARINATING AND COOLING TIME
COOK   ABOUT 40 MINUTES
SERVES   4

1 Combine the soy sauce, wine, brown sugar, garlic, and star anise in a zip-close plastic bag; add the lamb. Seal the bag; turn to coat the lamb. Refrigerate, turning the bag occasionally, at least 2 hours. Drain the lamb, reserving the marinade and discarding the star anise.

2 Meanwhile, cook the noodles according to package directions; drain. Transfer the noodles to an 8-inch round cake pan. Add the sesame oil; toss lightly and spread evenly to form a smooth cake. Let cool.

3 Heat 1 teaspoon of the peanut oil in a large nonstick skillet over medium-high heat. Invert the noodle cake into the skillet and cook until golden, about 2 minutes on each side. Transfer to a platter and keep warm.

4 Add 1 teaspoon of the peanut oil to the skillet, swirl to coat the pan, then add the lamb. Stir-fry until barely pink, 2–3 minutes. Transfer to a plate and keep warm.

5 Add the remaining 1 teaspoon peanut oil to the skillet, swirl to coat the pan, then add the scallions and ginger. Stir-fry until the scallions are softened, 2–3 minutes. Add the mushrooms and carrot; stir-fry until the carrot is softened, 6–8 minutes.

6 Stir in the cabbage, the marinade, and ¼ cup water; bring to a boil and cook until the cabbage is softened, about 2 minutes. Stir in the dissolved cornstarch and cook until the sauce is thickened, about 1 minute. Stir in the lamb and cook until heated through, about 1 minute. Pour the lamb mixture over the noodle cake.

PER SERVING (1 cup lamb mixture with ¼ of noodle cake): 289 Cal, 10 g Fat, 3 g Sat Fat, 1 g Trans Fat, 67 mg Chol, 362 mg Sod, 30 g Carb, 2 g Fib, 20 g Prot, 53 mg Calc. *POINTS* value: *6.*

- 2 tablespoons reduced-sodium soy sauce
- 1 tablespoon rice wine or dry sherry
- 2 teaspoons packed dark brown sugar
- 2 garlic cloves, minced
- 2 star anise or ¼ teaspoon ground anise
- 10 ounces boneless lamb shoulder or leg, trimmed and cut into 1-inch cubes
- ¼ pound thin egg noodles or spaghettini
- 1 teaspoon Asian (dark) sesame oil
- 3 teaspoons peanut oil
- 4 scallions, thinly sliced
- 1 (½-inch) piece peeled fresh ginger, minced
- 2 cups thinly sliced fresh mushrooms
- 1 carrot, cut into strips
- 1 cup thinly sliced napa cabbage
- 2 teaspoons cornstarch, dissolved in ¼ cup water

Noodle Cake with Lamb

Stir-Fried Noodles with Chicken, Mushrooms, and Leeks

Stir-Fried Noodles with Chicken, Mushrooms, and Leeks

PREP 15 MINUTES PLUS ABOUT 1 HOUR MARINATING AND STANDING TIME
COOK ABOUT 15 MINUTES
SERVES 4

1 Combine the wine, soy sauce, cornstarch, and sesame oil in a zip-close plastic bag; add the chicken. Seal the bag; turn to coat the chicken. Refrigerate, turning the bag occasionally, at least 30 minutes. Drain the chicken, reserving the marinade.

2 Meanwhile, place the noodles in a large bowl with enough hot water to cover. Let stand until softened, about 20 minutes; drain.

3 Heat a large nonstick skillet or wok over high heat until a drop of water sizzles. Add 2 teaspoons of the peanut oil, swirl to coat the pan, then add the chicken in batches. Stir-fry until no longer pink, 2–3 minutes. Transfer the chicken and pan juices to a plate and keep warm.

4 Add the remaining 1 teaspoon peanut oil to the skillet, swirl to coat the pan, then add the garlic and ginger. Stir-fry until just fragrant, about 15 seconds. Add the leeks, mushrooms, and bell pepper; stir-fry until the leeks are softened, 7–8 minutes. Add the broth and the marinade; bring to a boil. Stir in the chicken and noodles; cook, tossing gently, until the noodles have absorbed the sauce, 2–3 minutes.

PER SERVING (about 1½ cups): 232 Cal, 5 g Fat, 1 g Sat Fat, 0 g Trans Fat, 21 mg Chol, 152 mg Sod, 33 g Carb, 1 g Fib, 11 g Prot, 43 mg Calc. ***POINTS*** value: *5.*

HOW WE DID IT To clean the leeks thoroughly, trim the ends so about 5 inches remain. Slit each leek from top to bottom and wash well under cold, running water to remove any grit or sand that's trapped between its layers.

1 **tablespoon** rice wine or dry sherry

2 **teaspoons** reduced-sodium soy sauce

1 **teaspoon** cornstarch

1 **teaspoon** Asian (dark) sesame oil

5 **ounces** skinless boneless chicken breast, cut into 2 x ¼-inch strips

¼ **pound** thin rice stick noodles

3 **teaspoons** peanut oil

2 garlic cloves, minced

½ **teaspoon** minced peeled fresh ginger

2 leeks, trimmed to white and light-green parts, cleaned, and thinly sliced

1 **cup** thinly sliced fresh shiitake mushrooms

½ red bell pepper, seeded and diced

½ **cup** reduced-sodium chicken broth

Southwestern Skillet Macaroni and Cheese

PREP	10 MINUTES
COOK	ABOUT 25 MINUTES
SERVES	6

1 Cook the macaroni according to package directions omitting the salt, if desired; drain.

2 Meanwhile, spray a large nonstick skillet with nonstick spray and set over medium-high heat. Add the turkey and cook, breaking it up with a wooden spoon, until no longer pink, about 8 minutes. Stir in the onion, bell pepper, chili powder, cumin, and salt. Cook, stirring occasionally, until the onion is softened, about 3 minutes. Add the tomatoes, tomato sauce, chiles, and water, bring to a boil. Reduce the heat and simmer, stirring occasionally, until the flavors are blended, about 10 minutes. Add the macaroni and the cheese, stirring to combine.

PER SERVING (1 cup): 297 Cal, 13 g Fat, 5 g Sat Fat, 0 g Trans Fat, 73 mg Chol, 1,053 mg Sod, 22 g Carb, 3 g Fib, 22 g Prot, 198 mg Calc. **POINTS** value: *6.*

GOOD IDEA Serve this pasta with an assortment of garnishes, including diced white onion, sliced jalapeño pepper, and baked tortilla chips (6 tortilla chips for each serving will increase the **POINTS** value by 1).

1 cup elbow macaroni

1 pound ground skinless turkey breast

½ cup chopped onion

½ cup chopped green bell pepper

2 tablespoons chili powder

1 teaspoon ground cumin

½ teaspoon salt

1 (14½-ounce) can diced tomatoes, with their juice

1 (8-ounce) can tomato sauce

1 (4½-ounce) can chopped mild green chiles

½ cup water

1 cup shredded reduced-fat cheddar cheese (preferably extra-sharp)

Southwestern Skillet
Macaroni and Cheese

Wagon Wheels with Turkey Chili

PREP 10 MINUTES
COOK ABOUT 25 MINUTES
SERVES 6

1 Cook the pasta according to package directions omitting the salt, if desired; drain.

2 Meanwhile, heat the oil in a large nonstick skillet over medium-high heat. Add the onion, bell pepper, and garlic; cook, stirring frequently, until the vegetables are softened, about 2 minutes. Add the turkey and cook, breaking it up with a wooden spoon, until no longer pink, about 2 minutes. Stir in the tomatoes, tomato paste, chili powder, cumin, oregano, salt, and cayenne; bring to a boil. Reduce the heat and simmer, stirring occasionally, until thickened, about 15 minutes.

3 Serve the chili over the pasta.

PER SERVING (1 cup): 412 Cal, 12 g Fat, 3 g Sat Fat, 0 g Trans Fat, 60 mg Chol, 663 mg Sod, 54 g Carb, 5 g Fib, 23 g Prot, 88 mg Calc. ***POINTS*** value: **8.**

FOOD NOTE To make this a vegetarian dish, substitute 1 (15-ounce) can rinsed and drained red kidney or black beans for the turkey. Just add the beans with the tomatoes in step 2.

¾ **pound** wagon wheels pasta

1 **tablespoon** canola oil

1 **onion,** chopped

1 **green bell pepper,** seeded and chopped

2 **garlic cloves,** minced

1 **pound** ground skinless turkey

1 **(28-ounce) can** whole peeled tomatoes, drained and chopped

2 **tablespoons** tomato paste

1 **tablespoon** chili powder

2 **teaspoons** ground cumin

1 **teaspoon** dried oregano

¾ **teaspoon** salt

¼ **teaspoon** cayenne

Penne with Zucchini and Goat Cheese

PREP	10 MINUTES
COOK	ABOUT 25 MINUTES
SERVES	4

1 Cook the penne according to package directions omitting the salt, if desired. Drain, reserving ½ cup of the pasta cooking liquid, and keep warm.

2 Meanwhile, heat the oil in a large nonstick skillet over medium-high heat. Add the zucchini and salt; cook, stirring occasionally, until very soft, about 10 minutes. Stir in the penne and the reserved cooking liquid; cook, stirring frequently, until the liquid is slightly reduced. Reduce the heat and stir in the cheese; simmer, breaking the cheese up with a wooden spoon, until just melted, 1–2 minutes. Sprinkle with the mint and pepper.

PER SERVING (about 1 cup): 241 Cal, 9 g Fat, 4 g Sat Fat, 0 g Trans Fat, 10 mg Chol, 373 mg Sod, 32 g Carb, 1 g Fib, 9 g Prot, 45 mg Calc. *POINTS* value: *5.*

FOOD NOTE Chopped mint adds a refreshing flavor to this dish, although fresh chervil, tarragon, or thyme would be equally delicious.

1½ **cups penne**

1 **tablespoon olive oil**

2 **medium zucchini, thinly sliced**

½ **teaspoon salt**

3 **ounces goat cheese**

2 **teaspoons chopped fresh mint**

¼ **teaspoon freshly ground pepper**

Fettuccine with Sausage
and Arugula

Fettuccine with Sausage and Arugula

PREP 15 MINUTES
COOK ABOUT 25 MINUTES
SERVES 6

1 Cook the fettuccine according to package directions omitting the salt, if desired; drain.

2 Meanwhile, spray a large nonstick skillet with nonstick spray and set over medium-high heat. Add the sausage and cook, breaking it up with a wooden spoon, until browned, 3–4 minutes. Transfer to a plate.

3 Heat the oil in the skillet over medium heat. Add the mushrooms, onion, and garlic; cook, stirring frequently, until golden, about 10 minutes. Add the beans, broth, arugula, and the browned sausage; bring to a boil. Reduce the heat and simmer, covered, until the sausage is cooked through and the arugula is wilted, about 3 minutes. Stir in the tomato, basil, and pepper; cook until just heated through, about 2 minutes. Serve with the fettuccine.

PER SERVING (scant 1 cup sausage mixture and ⅔ cup fettuccine): 291 Cal, 7 g Fat, 1 g Sat Fat, 0 g Trans Fat, 27 mg Chol, 557 mg Sod, 41 g Carb, 8 g Fib, 19 g Prot, 83 mg Calc. *POINTS* value: *6.*

FOOD NOTE If you don't want to spend the extra money on shiitakes, this dish works equally well with regular white mushrooms.

½ **pound** whole-wheat fettuccine or spaghetti

½ **pound** sweet Italian turkey sausage

2 **teaspoons** extra-virgin olive oil

¼ **pound** fresh shiitake mushrooms, stems discarded, caps sliced

1 **small** onion, chopped

3 **garlic cloves,** minced

1 (15-ounce) **can** cannellini (white kidney) beans, rinsed and drained

1 **cup** reduced-sodium chicken broth

5 **ounces** arugula or spinach leaves (4 cups lightly packed)

1 **tomato,** chopped

¼ **cup chopped** fresh basil

¼ **teaspoon freshly** ground pepper

Penne with Cherry Tomatoes, Provolone, and Broccoli

PREP	10 MINUTES
COOK	ABOUT 25 MINUTES
SERVES	4

1 Cook the penne according to package directions omitting the salt, if desired and adding the broccoli to the pot during the last 2 minutes of cooking; drain.

2 Heat the oil in a large nonstick skillet over medium-high heat. Add the garlic and cook, stirring occasionally, until lightly golden, about 1 minute. Add the tomatoes and cook until the skins begin to blister slightly, about 1 minute. Add the penne and broccoli, the salt, and pepper; cook, stirring occasionally, until heated through, about 2 minutes. Transfer to a large bowl; stir in the provolone and Parmesan.

PER SERVING (1¾ cups): 338 Cal, 9 g Fat, 4 g Sat Fat, 0 g Trans Fat, 12 mg Chol, 559 mg Sod, 50 g Carb, 4 g Fib, 14 g Prot, 185 mg Calc. **POINTS** value: **7**.

FOOD NOTE Since provolone becomes much more robustly flavored as it ages, select an aged provolone for this dish.

½ **pound** penne

2½ **cups** fresh broccoli florets

1 **tablespoon** olive oil

3 **garlic cloves,** thinly sliced

1 **pint** cherry tomatoes

½ **teaspoon** salt

¼ **teaspoon coarsely ground black pepper**

2 **ounces sharp provolone cheese,** shredded

2 **tablespoons grated Parmesan cheese**

Lemon Capellini

PREP 5 MINUTES
COOK ABOUT 20 MINUTES
SERVES 4

1 Cook the capellini according to package directions omitting the salt, if desired; drain.

2 Heat the oil in a large skillet over medium-low heat. Add the garlic and cook, stirring frequently, until softened, 2–3 minutes. Add the capellini, parsley, lemon juice, and salt; toss to coat. Serve, sprinkled with pepper.

PER SERVING (about ¾ cup): 183 Cal, 3 g Fat, 0 g Sat Fat, 0 g Trans Fat, 0 mg Chol, 140 mg Sod, 33 g Carb, 1 g Fib, 6 g Prot, 16 mg Calc. **POINTS** value: **4.**

GOOD IDEA If you're looking for an extra kick, sprinkle one or two chopped anchovies (a little-known source of heart-healthy omega-3 fatty acids) over the capellini before serving.

6 ounces capellini

2 teaspoons olive oil

1–2 garlic cloves, minced

¼ cup minced fresh parsley

2 tablespoons fresh lemon juice

¼ teaspoon salt

Freshly ground pepper to taste

Gnocchi Marinara

PREP 10 MINUTES
COOK ABOUT 25 MINUTES
SERVES 4

1 Heat the oil in a large nonstick skillet over medium-high heat. Add the onion and cook, stirring frequently, until golden, about 5 minutes. Add the tomatoes, basil, garlic, and crushed red pepper. Cook until the sauce thickens, about 20 minutes.

2 Meanwhile, cook the gnocchi according to package directions; drain. Add the gnocchi to the sauce; toss to coat. Sprinkle with the cheese (if using).

PER SERVING (about 1 cup and ½ tablespoon cheese): 252 Cal, 17 g Fat, 6 g Sat Fat, 0 g Trans Fat, 81 mg Chol, 360 mg Sod, 14 g Carb, 1 g Fib, 12 g Prot, 278 mg Calc. *POINTS* value: *6.*

GOOD IDEA Use the ripest tomatoes you can find for this sauce, which also works well with a variety of pastas. Try the sauce with a chunky shape like shells or radiatore.

2 teaspoons olive oil

1 onion, chopped

2 tomatoes, peeled, seeded, and chopped

¼ cup chopped fresh basil

3 garlic cloves, crushed through a press

Pinch crushed red pepper

1 (16-ounce) package gnocchi

2 tablespoons grated Parmesan cheese (optional)

Gnocchi Marinara

Fusilli with Swiss Chard

PREP 15 MINUTES
COOK ABOUT 25 MINUTES
SERVES 4

1 Cook the fusilli according to package directions omitting the salt, if desired. Drain, reserving ¾ cup of the pasta cooking liquid, and keep warm.

2 Meanwhile, heat the oil in a large nonstick skillet over medium-high heat. Add the onion and cook, stirring occasionally, until softened, about 5 minutes. Add the chard, garlic, salt, and pepper; cook, stirring occasionally, until the chard is wilted, about 3 minutes. Add the tomato and cook, stirring occasionally, until the tomato is softened, 2–3 minutes. Stir in the fusilli and the reserved cooking liquid; cook, stirring frequently, until the chard is tender, about 2 minutes. Serve, sprinkled with the cheese.

PER SERVING (about 1 cup): 325 Cal, 4 g Fat, 1 g Sat Fat, 0 g Trans Fat, 1 mg Chol, 210 mg Sod, 60 g Carb, 6 g Fib, 13 g Prot, 141 mg Calc. **POINTS** value: *6.*

TRY IT Swiss chard is actually a type of beet that's grown for its broad, deep-green leaf, rather than for its root. Its flavor is milder than that of other cooking greens and is similar in taste to spinach. Reserve the stalks and use as you would celery in another recipe.

- 1½ cups **fusilli**
- 2 teaspoons **olive oil**
- 1 **onion**, chopped
- 1 bunch **Swiss chard**, cleaned and chopped
- 3 **garlic cloves**, minced
- ¼ teaspoon **salt**
- ¼ teaspoon freshly ground **pepper**
- 1 **tomato**, diced
- 4 teaspoons grated **Parmesan cheese**

Pasta with Chickpeas

PREP 10 MINUTES
COOK ABOUT 25 MINUTES
SERVES 4

1 Cook the pasta according to package directions omitting the salt, if desired. Drain, reserving ½ cup of the pasta cooking liquid, and keep warm.

2 Meanwhile, heat the oil in a large nonstick skillet over medium-high heat. Add the onions and cook, stirring occasionally, until softened, about 5 minutes. Stir in the chickpeas, tomatoes, parsley, garlic, crushed red pepper, and salt. Reduce the heat and simmer, stirring occasionally, until the tomatoes are softened, about 10 minutes. Stir in the pasta and the reserved cooking liquid; cook, stirring occasionally, until the sauce is slightly thickened, about 2 minutes.

PER SERVING (about 1½ cups): 259 Cal, 4 g Fat, 0 g Sat Fat, 0 g Trans Fat, 0 mg Chol, 228 mg Sod, 46 g Carb, 6 g Fib, 10 g Prot, 61 mg Calc. ***POINTS*** value: *5.*

FOOD NOTE If you're following the **Core Plan**, substitute whole-wheat penne for the pasta shells.

1½ cups medium pasta shells

2 teaspoons olive oil

2 onions, chopped

1 cup drained rinsed canned chickpeas

1 cup crushed tomatoes (no salt added)

2 tablespoons chopped fresh flat-leaf parsley

3 garlic cloves, minced

¼ teaspoon crushed red pepper

¼ teaspoon salt

Fettuccine with Creamy Spinach Sauce

PREP	10 MINUTES
COOK	ABOUT 20 MINUTES
SERVES	4

1 Cook the fettuccine according to package directions omitting the salt, if desired. Drain, reserving ½ cup of the pasta cooking liquid, and keep warm.

2 Meanwhile, heat the oil in a large nonstick skillet over medium-high heat. Add the onion and cook, stirring occasionally, until softened, about 5 minutes. Add the garlic and cook, stirring frequently, until fragrant, about 1 minute. Add the spinach, tomatoes, and salt; cook, stirring frequently, until the spinach is wilted, 4–5 minutes. Add the fettuccine, ¼ cup of the reserved cooking liquid, and the cheese. Cook, tossing the fettuccine, until just heated through; adding more of the remaining ¼ cup cooking liquid as necessary to make the sauce creamy. Serve, sprinkled with the pepper and nutmeg.

PER SERVING (about 1½ cups): 246 Cal, 6 g Fat, 2 g Sat Fat, 0 g Trans Fat, 9 mg Chol, 217 mg Sod, 39 g Carb, 3 g Fib, 11 g Prot, 140 mg Calc. *POINTS* value: *5.*

6 ounces fettuccine

2 teaspoons olive oil

½ onion, chopped

1 garlic clove, minced

2 cups chopped cleaned spinach

1 cup canned crushed tomatoes (no salt added)

¼ teaspoon salt

½ cup part-skim ricotta cheese, pureed

¼ teaspoon freshly ground pepper

Pinch freshly grated nutmeg

HOW WE DID IT Pureed ricotta cheese is a superb alternative to fat-laden heavy cream. To get the smoothest possible texture, be sure to puree the cheese in a blender.

Spaghetti with Tomatoes, Garlic, and Capers

PREP	10 MINUTES
COOK	ABOUT 25 MINUTES
SERVES	4

1 Cook the spaghetti according to package directions omitting the salt, if desired. Drain, reserving ¼ cup of the pasta cooking liquid, and keep warm.

2 Meanwhile, heat the oil in a large nonstick skillet over medium-high heat. Add the onion and cook, stirring occasionally, until softened, about 5 minutes. Add the tomatoes, capers, and garlic; cook, stirring occasionally, until the tomatoes are softened, 3–4 minutes. Add the spaghetti and the reserved cooking liquid; simmer until the liquid is slightly reduced, 1–2 minutes. Sprinkle with the parsley and pepper.

PER SERVING (about 1 cup): 228 Cal, 5 g Fat, 1 g Sat Fat, 0 g Trans Fat, 0 mg Chol, 170 mg Sod, 38 g Carb, 2 g Fib, 7 g Prot, 29 mg Calc. **POINTS** value: **5.**

6 ounces **spaghetti**

4 teaspoons **olive oil**

1 **onion**, diced

2 **tomatoes**, diced

2 tablespoons drained rinsed **capers**

4 **garlic cloves**, sliced

¼ cup chopped **fresh flat-leaf parsley**

½ teaspoon freshly **ground pepper**

FOOD NOTE If you don't have spaghetti on hand, try this dish with any long pasta except capellini—the delicate strands will overcook when you add them to the tomato mixture.

5 POINTS
(or fewer!)

CHAPTER 5

Oriental Pepper Steak

PREP 10 MINUTES
COOK ABOUT 15 MINUTES
SERVES 6

1 Heat a large nonstick skillet or wok over high heat until a drop of water sizzles. Add the oil, swirl to coat the pan, then add the steak. Stir-fry until lightly browned, about 4 minutes. Transfer to a bowl.

2 Add the onion and bell peppers to the skillet. Reduce the heat and cook, covered, until the vegetables are softened, about 6 minutes. Uncover and stir-fry until the vegetables are browned, about 4 minutes.

3 Meanwhile, whisk together the soy sauce and cornstarch in a medium bowl until smooth; whisk in the broth. Return the steak to the skillet, along with the soy sauce mixture. Cook, stirring occasionally, until the sauce boils and thickens, about 3 minutes.

PER SERVING (about 1¼ cups): 189 Cal, 10 g Fat, 4 g Sat Fat, 1 g Trans Fat, 39 mg Chol, 475 mg Sod, 8 g Carb, 1 g Fib, 17 g Prot, 13 mg Calc. **POINTS** value: **4.**

2 teaspoons canola oil

1 pound flank steak, trimmed and cut into thin strips

1 onion, cut into ¼-inch-thick slices

1 green bell pepper, cut into strips

½ yellow bell pepper, cut into strips

½ orange bell pepper, cut into strips

2 tablespoons reduced-sodium soy sauce

1½ tablespoons cornstarch

1¾ cups beef broth

HOW WE DID IT When slicing raw steak or other cuts of meat, always cut it across the grain. That will break up any fibers, making it more tender when cooked.

Oriental Pepper Steak

Spicy Tangerine Beef

PREP   15 MINUTES PLUS 1 HOUR MARINATING TIME
COOK   ABOUT 10 MINUTES
SERVES 4

1 Combine the soy sauce, wine, hoisin sauce, sesame oil, and ginger in a zip-close plastic bag; add the beef. Squeeze out the air and seal the bag; turn to coat the beef. Refrigerate, turning the bag occasionally, at least 1 hour. Drain the beef, reserving the marinade.

2 Heat a large nonstick skillet or wok over high heat until a drop of water sizzles. Add 1 teaspoon of the peanut oil, swirl to coat the pan, then add the beef. Stir-fry until barely pink, 1–2 minutes. Transfer the beef and the pan juices to a plate and keep warm.

3 Heat the remaining 1 teaspoon peanut oil in the skillet. Add the chile peppers and stir-fry until blackened, about 1 minute. Add the tangerine zest and stir-fry until fragrant, about 30 seconds. Add the snow peas, the beef, pan juices, and the reserved marinade; cook, stirring gently, about 2 minutes. Add the dissolved cornstarch and cook, stirring gently, until the sauce thickens and coats the beef, about 1 minute.

PER SERVING (about 1 cup): 162 Cal, 6 g Fat, 2 g Sat Fat, 1 g Trans Fat, 33 mg Chol, 239 mg Sod, 9 g Carb, 2 g Fiber, 15 g Prot, 39 mg Calc. **POINTS** value: **3.**

1 tablespoon **reduced-sodium soy sauce**

1 tablespoon **rice wine** or **dry sherry**

2 teaspoons **hoisin sauce**

1 teaspoon **Asian (dark) sesame oil**

½ teaspoon minced peeled **fresh ginger**

½ pound **boneless top round** or **sirloin steak,** trimmed and cut into 2-inch strips

2 teaspoons **peanut oil**

2 dried Szechuan **chile peppers,** seeds removed and discarded

Slivered zest of 1 small **tangerine** or **orange**

2 cups trimmed **fresh snow peas,** steamed

1 teaspoon **cornstarch,** dissolved in 2 tablespoons **water**

Crispy Beef with Water Chestnuts

PREP 10 MINUTES
COOK ABOUT 10 MINUTES
SERVES 4

1 Combine the steak, soy sauce, and cornstarch in a medium bowl; toss to coat.

2 Heat a large nonstick skillet or wok over high heat until a drop of water sizzles. Add 1 teaspoon of the oil, swirl to coat the pan, then add the scallions and bell pepper. Stir-fry until the bell pepper is softened, about 5 minutes. Transfer to a plate and keep warm.

3 Add the remaining 1 teaspoon oil to the skillet, swirl to coat the pan, then add the beef mixture. Stir-fry until just cooked through, 45–60 seconds. Stir in the vegetables, the water chestnuts, broth, and wine; cook, stirring gently, until heated through, about 2 minutes.

PER SERVING (about 1 cup): 174 Cal, 8 g Fat, 3 g Sat Fat, 1 g Trans Fat, 35 mg Chol, 210 mg Sod, 9 g Carb, 1 g Fiber, 15 g Prot, 18 mg Calc. **POINTS** value: **4.**

10 **ounces** flank steak, trimmed and thinly sliced

1 **tablespoon** reduced-sodium soy sauce

2 **teaspoons** cornstarch

2 **teaspoons** peanut oil

8 **scallions,** thinly sliced

½ **red bell pepper,** seeded and sliced

¾ **cup** water chestnuts, drained and sliced

2 **tablespoons** reduced-sodium beef broth

1 **tablespoon** rice wine or dry sherry

GOOD IDEA For a change of pace, serve this speedy stir-fry with whole-wheat couscous (⅔ cup cooked couscous for each serving will increase the **POINTS** value by 2).

Pork with Orange-Mustard Sauce

PREP   10 MINUTES
COOK   ABOUT 15 MINUTES
SERVES   4

1 Heat the oil in a medium skillet over medium-high heat. Add the pork and cook until browned, about 2 minutes on each side. Reduce the heat and cook, turning once, until no longer pink and cooked through, 4–6 minutes. Transfer the pork to a plate.

2 Add the broth, orange juice, salt, and pepper to the skillet; whisk in the mustard. Return the pork to the skillet; add the orange sections and cilantro and cook until heated through, 3–4 minutes.

PER SERVING (1 piece pork with about ½ cup sauce): 226 Cal, 11 g Fat, 3 g Sat Fat, 0 g Trans Fat, 63 mg Chol, 199 mg Sod, 7 g Carb, 1 g Fiber, 24 g Prot, 41 mg Calc. *POINTS* value: **5.**

ZAP IT For a super-easy side dish, pierce 1 pound small red potatoes with a fork. Place the potatoes and 2 tablespoons water in a large microwavable bowl. Cover with wax paper and microwave on High until tender, about 10 minutes; drain. Sprinkle with salt and pepper to taste (¼ pound cooked potatoes per serving will have a *POINTS* value of 2).

4 teaspoons vegetable oil

1 pound boneless pork loin, trimmed and cut into 4 equal pieces

½ cup reduced-sodium chicken broth

¼ cup orange juice

⅛ teaspoon salt

⅛ teaspoon freshly ground pepper

2 teaspoons Dijon mustard

1 cup peeled orange sections

1 tablespoon minced fresh cilantro

Pork and Bok Choy Stir-Fry

PREP 20 MINUTES
COOK ABOUT 5 MINUTES
SERVES 4

1 Whisk together the orange juice, soy sauce, cornstarch, vinegar, and sesame oil in a small bowl until smooth; set aside.

2 Heat a large nonstick skillet or wok over high heat until a drop of water sizzles. Add the vegetable oil, swirl to coat the pan, then add the pork. Stir-fry until browned, about 2 minutes. Transfer to a plate and keep warm.

3 Add the bok choy, bell pepper, scallions, garlic, ginger, and water to the skillet; stir-fry until the bok choy begins to wilt, 2–3 minutes. Add the orange juice mixture and stir until it coats the vegetables. Return the pork to the skillet and sprinkle with the salt and pepper; cook, stirring frequently, until heated through, 1–2 minutes. Remove the garlic and discard. Serve, sprinkled with the sesame seeds.

PER SERVING (about 1 cup): 197 Cal, 8 g Fat, 2 g Sat Fat, 0 g Trans Fat, 49 mg Chol, 592 mg Sod, 10 g Carb, 2 g Fiber, 20 g Prot, 72 mg Calc. **POINTS** value: **4.**

HOW WE DID IT To toast the sesame seeds, place them in a small, heavy, dry nonstick skillet; cook, shaking the pan constantly, until lightly browned, 2 to 3 minutes.

½ cup orange juice

2 tablespoons reduced-sodium soy sauce

2 teaspoons cornstarch

1 teaspoon white-wine vinegar

1 teaspoon Asian (dark) sesame oil

1 tablespoon vegetable oil

¾ pound pork tenderloin, trimmed and cut into thin strips

2 cups shredded bok choy leaves

1 red bell pepper, thinly sliced

2 scallions, sliced

2 garlic cloves, peeled and crushed

1 (½-inch) piece peeled fresh ginger, grated

3 tablespoons water

½ teaspoon salt

¼ teaspoon freshly ground pepper

1 teaspoon sesame seeds, toasted

Warm Cassoulet Salad

Warm Cassoulet Salad

PREP 15 MINUTES
COOK ABOUT 35 MINUTES
SERVES 6

1 Heat 2 teaspoons of the oil in a large skillet over medium-high heat. Add the pork and cook, stirring frequently, until browned, about 5 minutes. Add the onion and garlic; cook, stirring frequently, until the onion is softened, about 5 minutes. Add the wine, sun-dried tomatoes, thyme, and rosemary; bring just to a boil. Stir in the sausage and beans. Reduce the heat and simmer, covered, until the flavors are blended, about 15 minutes.

2 Stir in the cabbage and lemon zest. Increase the heat and cook, uncovered,, stirring occasionally, until the cabbage is slightly wilted, about 10 minutes. Stir in the parsley, salt, pepper, and the remaining 2 teaspoons oil. Serve at once.

PER SERVING (about 1½ cups): 253 Cal, 7 g Fat, 2 g Sat Fat, 0 g Trans Fat, 37 mg Chol, 935 mg Sod, 31 g Carb, 10 g Fiber, 20 g Prot, 140 mg Calc. **POINTS** value: **5.**

FOOD NOTE If you prefer home-cooked beans to canned, soak 1 cup dried beans overnight in enough water to cover by 2 inches; drain. To cook, cover with fresh water and boil until tender, about 1 hour.

4 teaspoons olive oil

½ pound pork tenderloin, trimmed and cut into ½-inch chunks

1 large white onion, chopped

4 large garlic cloves, minced

½ cup dry white wine

¼ cup sliced oil-packed sun-dried tomatoes, drained and patted dry

2 teaspoons fresh thyme leaves

2 teaspoons fresh rosemary leaves

¼ pound smoked turkey sausage, thinly sliced

2 (15-ounce) cans Great Northern beans, rinsed and drained

1 small red cabbage, thinly sliced

1 teaspoon grated lemon zest

2 tablespoons chopped fresh parsley

1 teaspoon salt

¼ teaspoon coarsely ground black pepper

Cider Pork Chops

PREP 10 MINUTES
COOK ABOUT 30 MINUTES
SERVES 4

1 Combine the flour, ¼ teaspoon of the pepper, and the salt in a large zip-close plastic bag. Add the pork chops, one at a time, and shake to coat.

2 Heat the oil in a large nonstick skillet over medium-high heat. Add the pork and cook until lightly browned, 1–2 minutes on each side. Reduce the heat and add the cider; simmer, covered, until the pork is cooked through and tender, 15–20 minutes. With a slotted spatula, transfer the pork to a platter; keep warm.

3 Add the vinegar and lemon zest to the pan juices; bring to a boil. Cook, stirring occasionally, until slightly thickened, about 5 minutes; stir in the remaining ¼ teaspoon pepper. Pour the sauce over the pork.

PER SERVING (1 chop with about 1 tablespoon sauce): 231 Cal, 10 g Fat, 3 g Sat Fat, 0 g Trans Fat, 73 mg Chol, 188 mg Sod, 8 g Carb, 0 g Fiber, 22 g Prot, 10 mg Calc. *POINTS* value: *5.*

HOW WE DID IT Don't be tempted to overcook the pork; it's best when cooked to medium doneness (160°F on a meat thermometer). Correctly cooked pork is juicy and tender, with a slight blush of pink in the center.

3 tablespoons
   all-purpose flour

½ teaspoon freshly
   ground pepper

¼ teaspoon salt

4 (¼-pound) boneless
   center-cut pork loin
   chops, trimmed

2 teaspoons
   vegetable oil

½ cup apple cider

1 tablespoon apple-
   cider vinegar

1 teaspoon grated
   lemon zest

Cider Pork Chops

Chicken and Ham "Pot Pie"

PREP 15 MINUTES
COOK ABOUT 30 MINUTES
SERVES 8

1 Preheat the oven to 400°F. Prepare the biscuits according to package directions.

2 Meanwhile, melt the butter in a large nonstick skillet over medium-high heat. Add the chicken and ham; cook, stirring occasionally, until the chicken is almost cooked through, about 6 minutes. Add the mixed vegetables, onion, and garlic. Cook until the vegetables are tender, about 4 minutes. Stir in the broth, thyme, and pepper; cook about 2 minutes.

3 Dissolve the cornstarch in the milk and stir into the skillet; bring to a boil and cook until thickened, about 1 minute. Top the filling with the biscuits and serve.

PER SERVING (1½ cups): 225 Cal, 6 g Fat, 2 g Sat Fat, 1 g Trans Fat, 68 mg Chol, 760 mg Sod, 22 g Carb, 2 g Fib, 20 g Prot, 53 mg Calc. **POINTS** value: **5.**

FOOD NOTE Chicken thighs are moist and flavorful in this dish, but if you prefer white meat, substitute an equal amount of skinless boneless chicken breast (you'll reduce the per-serving **POINTS** value by 1).

1 (7½-ounce) package refrigerated buttermilk biscuits

1 tablespoon butter

1 pound skinless boneless chicken thighs, cut into 1-inch cubes

1 (½-pound) boneless ham steak, cut into ½-inch cubes

1 (10-ounce) package frozen mixed vegetables

1 onion, chopped

2 garlic cloves, minced

1 cup reduced-sodium chicken broth

1 teaspoon dried thyme

½ teaspoon coarsely ground black pepper

2 tablespoons cornstarch

¾ cup low-fat (2%) milk

Curried Turkey Stir-Fry

PREP 20 MINUTES PLUS 30 MINUTES MARINATING TIME
COOK ABOUT 30 MINUTES
SERVES 4

1 Combine the soy sauce and sesame oil in a zip-close plastic bag; add the turkey. Squeeze out the air and seal the bag; turn to coat the turkey. Refrigerate, turning the bag occasionally, at least 30 minutes. Drain the turkey, reserving the marinade.

2 Heat a large nonstick skillet or wok over high heat until a drop of water sizzles. Add 1 teaspoon of the peanut oil, swirl to coat the pan, then add the turkey. Stir-fry until cooked through, 3–4 minutes. Transfer the turkey and pan juices to a plate and keep warm.

3 Add the remaining 1 teaspoon peanut oil to the skillet, swirl to coat the pan, then add the onion. Stir-fry until softened, about 5 minutes. Sprinkle with the curry powder and stir-fry until fragrant, about 30 seconds. Add the turkey, cauliflower, carrot, peas, broth, the reserved marinade, and the dissolved cornstarch; bring to a boil. Reduce the heat and simmer until the sauce thickens and coats the turkey, 1–2 minutes.

PER SERVING (about 1¾ cups): 171 Cal, 5 g Fat, 1 g Sat Fat, 0 g Trans Fat, 35 mg Chol, 248 mg Sod, 15 g Carb, 5 g Fiber, 19 g Prot, 58 mg Calc. **POINTS** value: **3.**

GOOD IDEA Serve this soul-warming curry with toasted pita bread (1 small plain or whole-wheat pita bread for each serving will increase the **POINTS** value by 1).

1 tablespoon reduced-sodium soy sauce

1 teaspoon Asian (dark) sesame oil

½ pound skinless boneless turkey breast, cut into thin strips

2 teaspoons peanut oil

½ onion, finely diced

1 tablespoon curry powder

3 cups chopped fresh cauliflower florets, steamed

1 carrot, cut into thin strips and steamed

1 cup thawed frozen peas

½ cup reduced-sodium chicken broth

1 teaspoon cornstarch, dissolved in 1 tablespoon water

Sweet-and-Sour Turkey

PREP 15 MINUTES PLUS ABOUT 1 HOUR MARINATING AND STANDING TIME
COOK ABOUT 35 MINUTES
SERVES 4

1 Combine 1 tablespoon of the soy sauce and the wine in a zip-close plastic bag; add the turkey. Seal the bag; turn to coat the turkey. Refrigerate about 30 minutes. Drain; discard any marinade.

2 Combine mushrooms and 1 cup boiling water in a bowl. Cover, let stand until softened, 20 minutes. Drain; thinly slice the mushrooms. Coat the turkey in 1/4 cup cornstarch, one piece at a time, shaking off the excess.

3 Heat 1 teaspoon of the oil in a large nonstick skillet over medium-high heat. Add half the turkey and cook, stirring gently, until cooked through, 4–5 minutes. Transfer to a serving platter; keep warm. Repeat with 1 teaspoon of the oil and the remaining turkey.

4 Heat 1 teaspoon of the oil in the skillet. Add the bell peppers, carrot, and onion; cook, stirring, until very tender, 10–12 minutes. Transfer to a plate; keep warm.

5 Heat the remaining 1 teaspoon oil in the skillet. Add the mushrooms, pineapple, scallions, garlic, and ginger; cook, stirring, until the pineapple is lightly browned, 4–5 minutes. Stir in the reserved vegetables; set aside.

6 Whisk 1 tablespoon water and the remaining 2 teaspoons cornstarch in a bowl. Bring 1/4 cup water, the sugar, vinegar, and the remaining 1 tablespoon soy sauce to a boil in a saucepan. Stir in the dissolved cornstarch; cook, stirring, until the sauce thickens. Pour the sauce over the vegetables and bring to a boil. Pour the vegetable mixture over the turkey and toss.

PER SERVING (about 1 1/2 cups): 256 Cal, 5 g Fat, 1 g Sat Fat, 0 g Trans Fat, 44 mg Chol, 350 mg Sod, 32 g Carb, 3 g Fiber, 19 g Prot, 37 mg Calc. **POINTS** value: **5.**

2 tablespoons reduced-sodium soy sauce

1 tablespoon rice wine

10 ounces skinless boneless turkey breast

5 dried Chinese black mushroom caps (about 1/2 ounce)

1/4 cup + 2 teaspoons cornstarch

4 teaspoons peanut oil

1 green bell pepper, cut into 1-inch pieces

1 red bell pepper, cut into 1-inch pieces

1 carrot, thinly sliced

1 onion, cut into 1-inch cubes

1/2 cup drained canned unsweetened pineapple chunks

4 scallions, cut into 1-inch lengths

2 garlic cloves, peeled and crushed

1 (1/2-inch) piece peeled fresh ginger, minced

2 tablespoons sugar

2 tablespoons red-wine vinegar

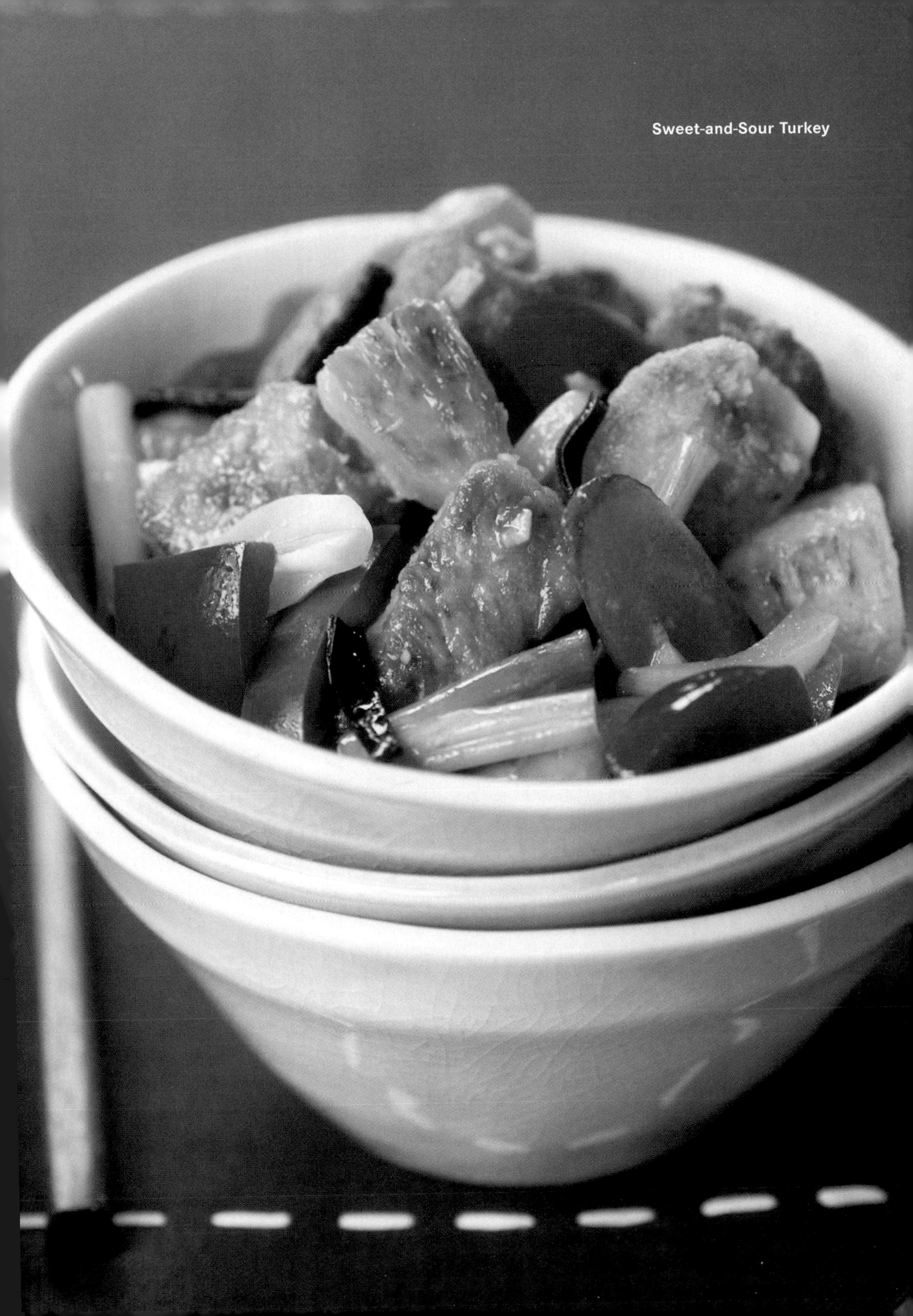
Sweet-and-Sour Turkey

Piedmontese Braised Turkey

PREP 10 MINUTES
COOK ABOUT 25 MINUTES
SERVES 6

1 Bring the broth and wine to a boil in a medium nonstick skillet; boil 2 minutes. Add the turkey, onion, and sage. Reduce the heat and simmer, covered, until the turkey is cooked through, about 15 minutes. Remove the skillet from the heat.

2 To make the gravy, whisk together ¼ cup of the braising liquid and the cornstarch in a small bowl until smooth. Transfer 1 cup of the braising liquid to a small saucepan; bring to a boil. Remove the saucepan from the heat and whisk in the dissolved cornstarch. Return the saucepan to the heat and cook until the gravy is thickened and translucent, about 2 minutes. Stir in the salt and pepper.

3 Transfer the turkey from the remaining braising liquid to a cutting board; cut into 12 slices. With a slotted spoon, scatter each serving with the onion, then drizzle with the gravy.

2 **cups** reduced-sodium chicken broth

1 **cup** dry red wine

1½ **pounds** turkey breast tenderloin

1 **small** red onion, thinly sliced

2 **tablespoons** chopped fresh sage

1 **tablespoon** cornstarch

½ **teaspoon** salt

¼ **teaspoon** freshly ground pepper

PER SERVING (2 slices turkey with about 3 tablespoons gravy): 177 Cal, 2 g Fat, 1 g Sat Fat, 0 g Trans Fat, 72 mg Chol, 289 mg Sod, 4 g Carb, 1 g Fiber, 29 g Prot, 36 mg Calc. **POINTS** value: **4.**

GOOD IDEA This dish is excellent with roasted Brussels sprouts. Here's how: Toss 4 cups trimmed sprouts, 2 teaspoons olive oil, and salt and pepper to taste. Spread on a baking sheet and roast in a preheated 450°F oven until browned, about 20 minutes, shaking the pan a few times so that the sprouts brown evenly. (1 cup cooked Brussels sprouts will increase the **POINTS** value per serving by ½.)

Turkey Sausage Fajitas

PREP 5 MINUTES
COOK ABOUT 15 MINUTES
SERVES 4

1 Heat the oil in a large nonstick skillet over medium-high heat. Add the sausage and cook, stirring frequently, until browned, about 5 minutes. Add the bell peppers and onion; cook, covered, stirring occasionally, until the vegetables are tender, about 10 minutes.

2 Spoon the sausage mixture down the center of each tortilla and roll the tortilla up around the filling.

PER SERVING (1 fajita): 227 Cal, 7 g Fat, 2 g Sat Fat, 0 g Trans Fat, 30 mg Chol, 718 mg Sod, 29 g Carb, 11 g Fib, 13 g Prot, 57 mg Calc. **POINTS** value: **4.**

ZAP IT An easy way to heat tortillas is to loosely wrap them in plastic wrap and microwave on High 1 minute. To keep them soft and warm, cover the warm tortillas until ready to serve.

1 teaspoon canola oil

½ pound Italian turkey sausage, cut into ½-inch-thick slices

2 green bell peppers, seeded and sliced

1 large onion, thinly sliced

4 (8-inch) low-fat flour tortillas, warmed

Turkey Cutlets with
Cranberry-Pear Chutney

Turkey Cutlets with Cranberry-Pear Chutney

PREP 10 MINUTES
COOK ABOUT 10 MINUTES
SERVES 4

1 Whisk together the brown sugar, broth, vinegar, orange juice, cinnamon, ginger, and cloves in a small bowl; set aside.

2 Sprinkle the cutlets with the salt and pepper. Heat the oil in a large nonstick skillet over medium-high heat. Add the cutlets and cook until cooked through, about 3 minutes on each side. Transfer to a plate and keep warm.

3 Add the pear, cranberries, and the sugar mixture to the skillet; bring to a boil. Simmer, uncovered, until the berries begin to pop and the chutney thickens, about 5 minutes. Spoon the chutney over the cutlets.

PER SERVING (1 cutlet with about ½ cup chutney): 260 Cal, 3 g Fat, 1 g Sat Fat, 0 g Trans Fat, 66 mg Chol, 402 mg Sod, 30 g Carb, 2 g Fib, 27 g Prot, 42 mg Calc. **POINTS** value: **5.**

EXPRESS LANE If you're really pressed for time, use two drained canned pear halves in juice instead of fresh pear for the chutney.

6 tablespoons packed light brown sugar

¼ cup reduced-sodium chicken broth

¼ cup apple-cider vinegar

2 tablespoons orange juice

¼ teaspoon cinnamon

¼ teaspoon ground ginger

Pinch ground cloves

4 (¼-pound) turkey cutlets

½ teaspoon salt

¼ teaspoon coarsely ground black pepper

1 teaspoon canola oil

1 ripe pear, peeled and chopped

1 cup fresh or frozen cranberries

Beer-Braised Kielbasa with Sautéed Onions

PREP	10 MINUTES
COOK	ABOUT 40 MINUTES
SERVES	6

1 Heat the oil in a large nonstick skillet over medium-high heat. Add the onions and sugar; cook, stirring occasionally, until lightly browned, about 10 minutes. Push the onions to the center of the skillet and place the kielbasa around them; cook, stirring the onions occasionally, until the kielbasa is lightly browned, about 5 minutes on each side.

2 Pour in the beer; bring to a boil. Reduce the heat and simmer until the kielbasa is heated through, about 10 minutes on each side. Transfer the kielbasa and onions to a platter and keep warm. Increase the heat and boil the sauce until it is reduced and syrupy, 3–5 minutes. Serve on the side.

PER SERVING (⅙ of kielbasa with about ⅓ cup onions and 1 tablespoon sauce): 166 Cal, 4 g Fat, 1 g Sat Fat, 0 g Trans Fat, 34 mg Chol, 803 mg Sod, 15 g Carb, 2 g Fiber, 12 g Prot, 22 mg Calc. **POINTS** value: **3.**

GOOD IDEA Serve this hearty fare with mashed potatoes or egg noodles (½ cup mashed potatoes or cooked noodles for each serving will increase the **POINTS** value by 2).

2 teaspoons canola oil

4 onions, thinly sliced

½ teaspoon sugar

1 pound reduced-fat turkey kielbasa, lightly scored

1 (12-ounce) bottle beer

Curried Fried Rice

PREP 10 MINUTES
COOK ABOUT 15 MINUTES
SERVES 4

1 Place the rice in a shallow bowl; with moistened fingers, stir the rice to separate the grains.

2 Heat a large nonstick skillet or wok over high heat until a drop of water sizzles. Add the oil, swirl to coat the pan, then add the scallions. Stir-fry until softened, 2–3 minutes. Add the curry powder and stir-fry until just fragrant, about 30 seconds. Add the carrots, green beans, and ham; stir-fry until heated through, about 1 minute. Stir in the rice and water; cook, tossing gently to combine, until the rice is thoroughly coated and heated through.

PER SERVING (about 1 cup): 239 Cal, 6 g Fat, 1 g Sat Fat, 0 g Trans Fat, 9 mg Chol, 165 mg Sod, 40 g Carb, 3 g Fiber, 7 g Prot, 56 mg Calc. **POINTS** value: **5.**

FOOD NOTE Use leftover rice from Chinese take-out or if you want to cook the rice yourself, you'll need to start with 1 cup uncooked long-grain white or brown rice.

3 cups cold cooked long-grain white rice or brown rice

4 teaspoons peanut oil

8 scallions, thinly sliced

2 teaspoons curry powder

2 carrots, diced and steamed

1 cup steamed chopped fresh green beans

½ cup lean turkey ham

2 tablespoons water

Rice Pancakes with Shrimp

PREP	20 MINUTES
COOK	ABOUT 10 MINUTES
SERVES	4

1 Puree the rice, milk, egg, flour, soy sauce, and sesame oil in a food processor or blender to make a smooth, thin batter. Add the baking soda and pulse once or twice to blend.

2 Heat the peanut oil in a small nonstick skillet over medium-high heat. Add the scallions and cook, stirring frequently, until softened, 2–3 minutes. Stir the scallions into the batter, then stir in the shrimp.

3 Spray the skillet with nonstick spray and set over medium-high heat. Pour one-quarter of the batter into the skillet, tilting to cover the bottom of the skillet. Cook until the underside is set, about 1 minute. Carefully turn over and cook the other side until lightly browned, 30–45 seconds. Slide the pancake onto a plate and keep warm. Repeat with the remaining batter, spraying the skillet with nonstick spray between each batch, to make 4 pancakes. Sprinkle the pancakes with the cilantro.

PER SERVING (1 pancake): 146 Cal, 5 g Fat, 1 g Sat Fat, 0 g Trans Fat, 110 mg Chol, 403 mg Sod, 14 g Carb, 0 g Fiber, 10 g Prot, 64 mg Calc. **POINTS** value: **3.**

GOOD IDEA Enjoy these pancakes plain or with a sprinkling of reduced-sodium soy sauce. The recipe doubles easily.

½ cup cooked white rice

½ cup low-fat (1%) milk

1 large egg

3 tablespoons all-purpose flour

1 tablespoon reduced-sodium soy sauce

1 teaspoon Asian (dark) sesame oil

½ teaspoon baking soda

1 teaspoon peanut oil

4 scallions, sliced

¼ pound small shrimp, cooked, peeled, and halved lengthwise

1 tablespoon minced fresh cilantro

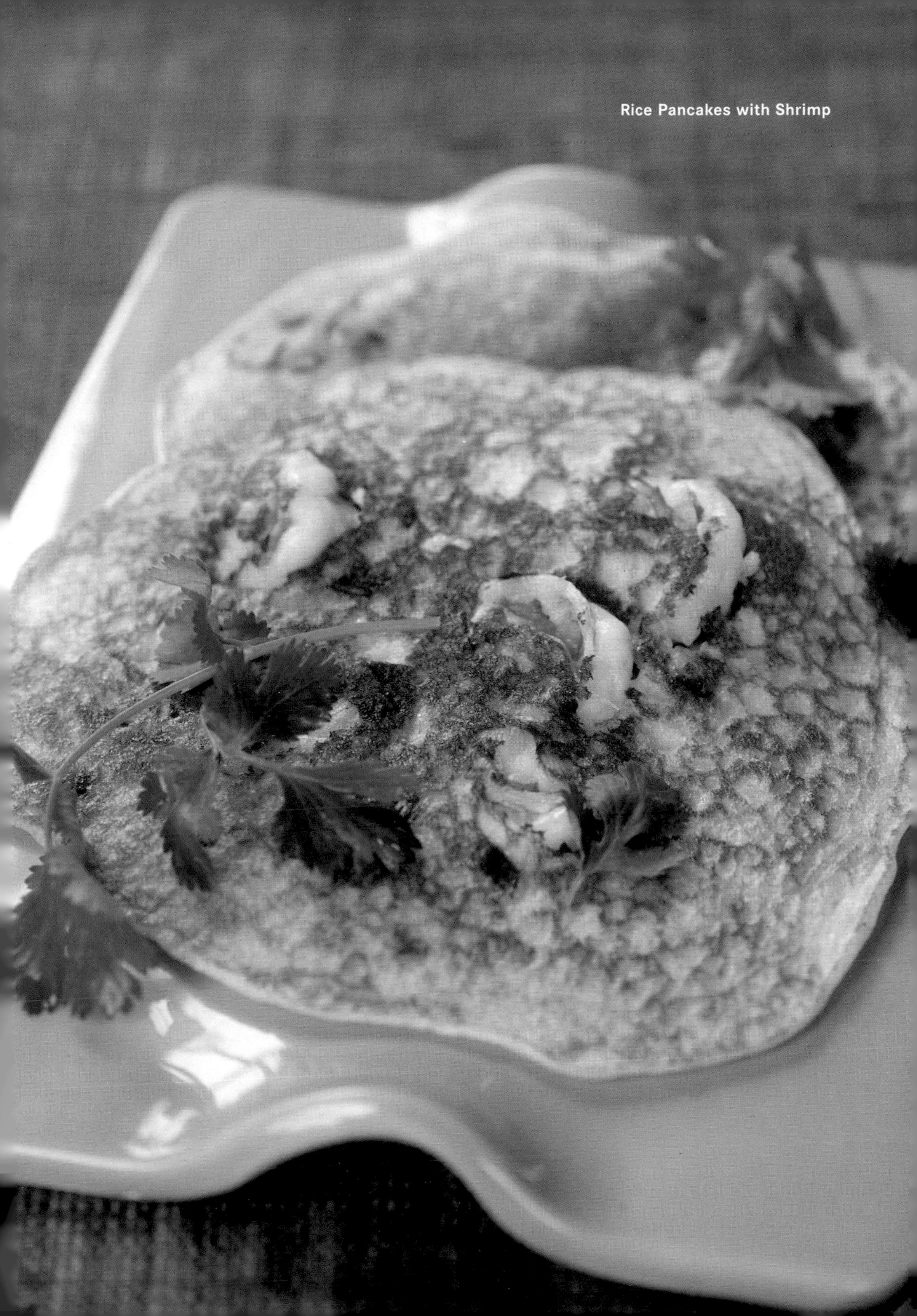
Rice Pancakes with Shrimp

Shrimp, Pork, and Broccoli Stir-Fry

PREP 15 MINUTES PLUS 1 HOUR MARINATING TIME
COOK ABOUT 25 MINUTES
SERVES 4

1 Combine the soy sauce, wine, ginger, and hoisin sauce in a zip-close plastic bag; add the pork. Squeeze out the air and seal the bag; turn to coat the pork. Refrigerate, turning the bag occasionally, at least 1 hour. Drain the pork, reserving the marinade.

2 Meanwhile, whisk together the broth and cornstarch in a small bowl until smooth; set aside.

3 Heat a large nonstick skillet or wok over high heat. Add 1 teaspoon of the oil, swirl to coat the pan, then add the chili paste. Stir-fry until fragrant, about 10 seconds. Add the shrimp and stir-fry until barely pink, 1–2 minutes. Transfer to a plate and keep warm.

4 Add 1 teaspoon of the oil to the skillet, swirl to coat the pan, then add the pork. Stir-fry until no longer pink, 2–3 minutes. Transfer the pork and pan juices to the plate with the shrimp and keep warm.

5 Add the remaining 1 teaspoon oil to the skillet, swirl to coat the pan, then add the scallions and garlic. Stir-fry until softened, 3–4 minutes. Stir in the broccoli, carrots, and the reserved marinade; bring to a boil and cook, stirring occasionally, about 1 minute. Stir in the pork, shrimp, and the broth mixture; cook, stirring occasionally, until the sauce thickens, 2–3 minutes.

PER SERVING (about 1 cup): 205 Cal, 7 g Fat, 2 g Sat Fat, 0 g Trans Fat, 107 mg Chol, 345 mg Sod, 13 g Carb, 4 g Fiber, 23 g Prot, 87 mg Calc. **POINTS** value: **4.**

- 1 tablespoon reduced-sodium soy sauce
- 1 tablespoon rice wine or dry sherry
- 1 teaspoon minced peeled fresh ginger
- 1 teaspoon hoisin sauce
- ¼ pound boneless pork loin, cut into thin strips
- ½ cup reduced-sodium chicken broth
- 2 teaspoons cornstarch
- 3 teaspoons peanut oil
- ½ teaspoon hot chili paste
- ½ pound medium shrimp, peeled and deveined
- 4 scallions, thinly sliced
- 1 garlic clove, minced
- 2 cups fresh broccoli florets, steamed
- 2 carrots, cut into thin strips and steamed

GOOD IDEA Serve this spicy stir-fry over a bed of whole-wheat linguine (⅔ cup cooked pasta for each serving will increase the **POINTS** value by 2).

Five-Spice Tofu Stir-Fry

PREP 20 MINUTES PLUS ABOUT 3 ½ HOURS STANDING AND MARINATING TIME
COOK ABOUT 20 MINUTES
SERVES 4

1 Place the tofu between 2 flat plates. Weight the top plate with a heavy can or a cast-iron skillet until the tofu bulges at the sides but does not split. Let stand about 30 minutes, then pour off the water that has accumulated. Cut the tofu into ³/₄-inch cubes.

2 Combine the soy sauce, tangerine zest, vinegar, five-spice powder, chili paste, ginger, and garlic in a zip-close plastic bag; add the tofu. Seal the bag; turn to coat the tofu. Refrigerate, turning the bag occasionally, at least 3 hours. Drain the tofu, reserving the marinade.

3 Heat a large nonstick skillet or wok over high heat until a drop of water sizzles. Add 2 teaspoons of the oil, swirl to coat the pan, then add the tofu. Stir-fry until lightly browned, 3–4 minutes. Transfer the tofu to a plate and keep warm.

4 Add the remaining 1 teaspoon oil to the skillet, swirl to coat the pan, then add the scallions and bell pepper. Stir-fry until softened, about 5 minutes. Add the snow peas, water chestnuts, the tofu, ¹/₃ cup water, and the marinade; cook, tossing gently, until heated through, about 2 minutes. Add the dissolved cornstarch and cook, stirring, until the sauce thickens, about 1 minute.

PER SERVING (about 1½ cups): 117 Cal, 4 g Fat, 1 g Sat Fat, 0 g Trans Fat, 0 mg Chol, 372 mg Sod, 14 g Carb, 2 g Fiber, 6 g Prot, 55 mg Calc. **POINTS** value: **2.**

TRY IT Five-spice powder is an aromatic mixture that usually includes ground cinnamon, cloves, fennel seeds, nutmeg, star anise, and sometimes Szechuan peppercorns. You can find it in Asian markets or the spice aisle of the supermarket.

½ **pound** reduced-fat firm tofu

2 **tablespoons** reduced-sodium soy sauce

1 **tablespoon grated** tangerine or orange zest

1 **tablespoon** white vinegar

1 **teaspoon** five-spice powder

½ **teaspoon** hot chili paste

1 **(1-inch) piece peeled** fresh ginger, **minced**

1 **garlic clove, minced**

3 **teaspoons** peanut oil

8 **scallions, thinly sliced**

½ **red bell pepper, seeded and cut into 1-inch pieces**

1 **cup trimmed** fresh snow peas, **steamed**

³/₄ **cup** water chestnuts, **drained and sliced**

2 **teaspoons** cornstarch, **dissolved in 1 tablespoon** water

Potato and Pepper Frittata

Potato and Pepper Frittata

PREP 15 MINUTES
COOK ABOUT 15 MINUTES
SERVES 4

1 Heat the oil in a medium nonstick skillet over medium heat. Add the potatoes, scallions, bell pepper, and salt; cook, stirring frequently, until the vegetables are tender and golden, 8–10 minutes. Stir in the parsley.

2 Meanwhile, spray a large nonstick skillet with nonstick spray and set over medium heat. Add the egg substitute and cook until set, 7–8 minutes, lifting the edges frequently with a spatula to let the uncooked egg flow underneath.

3 Spoon the potato mixture over the frittata, then sprinkle with the cheddar, Parmesan, and ground pepper. Cover the skillet and cook until the cheeses melt, about 3 minutes.

PER SERVING (¼ of frittata): 190 Cal, 4 g Fat, 1 g Sat Fat, 0 g Trans Fat, 1 mg Chol, 653 mg Sod, 26 g Carb, 4 g Fib, 13 g Prot, 98 mg Calc. **POINTS** value: **3.**

GOOD IDEA For a browned cheese topping, pop the frittata under a hot broiler 2 to 3 minutes. If the handle on your skillet is not flameproof, cover it with heavy-duty foil.

1 tablespoon canola oil

2 cups (from a 32-ounce bag) frozen hash-brown potatoes

1 bunch scallions, thinly sliced

1 red bell pepper, seeded and chopped

¾ teaspoon salt

¼ cup chopped fresh flat-leaf parsley

2 cups fat-free egg substitute

½ cup shredded reduced-fat cheddar cheese

1 tablespoon grated Parmesan cheese

½ teaspoon coarsely ground black pepper

Broccoli Rabe and Rice Frittata

PREP	15 MINUTES
COOK	ABOUT 25 MINUTES
SERVES	6

1 Preheat the broiler.

2 Heat the oil in a large nonstick skillet with an ovenproof handle over medium-high heat, tilting the pan so that the oil covers the sides. Add the onions and cook, stirring occasionally, until softened, about 5 minutes. Add the broccoli rabe, garlic, crushed red pepper, and fennel seeds; cook until the broccoli rabe is wilted, about 3 minutes. Add the rice; toss to combine.

3 Meanwhile, whisk together the eggs, egg whites, cheese, ground pepper, and salt in a medium bowl.

4 Pour the egg mixture over the rice mixture and smooth over with a spatula. Reduce the heat to low; cook, lifting the sides of the frittata to allow the egg mixture to flow underneath, until the eggs are almost set, about 10 minutes. Place the frittata in the skillet under the broiler and broil until the egg mixture is set and the top is golden, 2–3 minutes. Slide the frittata onto a plate and cut into 6 wedges.

PER SERVING (1 wedge): 211 Cal, 9 g Fat, 3 g Sat Fat, 0 g Trans Fat, 217 mg Chol, 423 mg Sod, 18 g Carb, 3 g Fiber, 14 g Prot, 155 mg Calc. **POINTS** value: *4.*

TRY IT Broccoli rabe, a vegetable related to both the cabbage and turnip family, is an intense, somewhat bitter green popular in Italian and Chinese cooking. It is high in vitamins yet low in calories and adds a wonderful sharp taste to this frittata.

2 teaspoons olive oil

2 onions, chopped

2½ cups chopped broccoli rabe

3 garlic cloves, minced

½ teaspoon crushed red pepper

½ teaspoon fennel seeds

1½ cups cooked brown rice

6 large eggs

3 egg whites

½ cup grated Parmesan cheese

½ teaspoon freshly ground pepper

½ teaspoon salt

Portobello Burgers

PREP	5 MINUTES
COOK	ABOUT 15 MINUTES
SERVES	4

1 Brush the mushrooms with 2 teaspoons of the oil and sprinkle with the salt and pepper.

2 Heat 2 teaspoons of the oil in a large nonstick skillet over medium-high heat. Add the mushrooms and cook, covered, until browned and tender, about 6 minutes on each side. Transfer to a plate and keep warm.

3 Heat the remaining 2 teaspoons oil in the skillet. Add the garlic, oregano, and basil; cook, stirring constantly, until fragrant, about 30 seconds. Add the vinegar and cook until slightly syrupy, about 2 minutes. Add the mushrooms and turn to coat.

4 Spread half of each muffin with 1½ teaspoons of the mustard; layer with a lettuce leaf, tomato slice, and mushroom. Cover with the remaining muffin halves.

PER SERVING (1 burger): 256 Cal, 8 g Fat, 1 g Sat Fat, 0 g Trans Fat, 0 mg Chol, 601 mg Sod, 35 g Carb, 6 g Fib, 9 g Prot, 178 mg Calc. **POINTS** value: **5.**

4 fresh Portobello mushrooms, stems discarded

6 teaspoons olive oil

½ teaspoon salt

¼ teaspoon coarsely ground black pepper

2 garlic cloves, minced

1 teaspoon dried oregano

1 teaspoon dried basil

¼ cup balsamic vinegar

4 English muffins, split and toasted

2 tablespoons Dijon mustard

4 lettuce leaves

4 slices tomato

GOOD IDEA Portobello burgers are lean enough to allow for an indulgence—serve with some blue cheese and fresh pear slices (1 tablespoon crumbled blue cheese for each serving will increase the **POINTS** value by 1).

Western Omelette

PREP   10 MINUTES
COOK   ABOUT 10 MINUTES
SERVES   2

1 Melt the butter in a medium nonstick skillet over medium heat. Add the onion, bell pepper, ham, thyme, and ground pepper; cook, stirring occasionally, until the vegetables soften, 4–5 minutes.

2 Pour in the egg substitute and swirl to cover the pan. Cook, stirring gently, until the underside begins to set, about 3 minutes. Fold one side of the omelette over the other and cook about 2 minutes. Turn over and cook until cooked through, about 1 minute. Slide the omelette onto a serving plate.

PER SERVING (½ omelette): 179 Cal, 5 g Fat, 2 g Sat Fat, 0 g Trans Fat, 37 mg Chol, 974 mg Sod, 5 g Carb, 1 g Fib, 27 g Prot, 50 mg Calc. *POINTS* value: *4.*

HOW WE DID IT For the best results when making an omelette, use a heavy nonstick skillet with curved sides, so that the omelette will easily slide onto a plate.

1 teaspoon butter

¼ cup chopped onion

¼ cup chopped green bell pepper

¼ pound deli-sliced ham, chopped

¼ teaspoon dried thyme

⅛ teaspoon coarsely ground black pepper

1 cup fat-free egg substitute

Vegetable and Quinoa Sauté with Orange

PREP 10 MINUTES
COOK ABOUT 40 MINUTES
SERVES 4

1 Cook the quinoa according to package directions.

2 Meanwhile, heat the oil in a large nonstick skillet over medium-high heat. Add the onion and cook, stirring frequently, until softened, about 5 minutes. Add the carrots, garlic, and cumin; cook, stirring occasionally, until the carrots are wilted, about 2 minutes.

3 Stir in the quinoa, chickpeas, orange juice, raisins, salt, and cinnamon; cook, covered, until the juice is absorbed and the flavors are blended, about 10 minutes. Stir in the cilantro.

PER SERVING (about 1 cup): 205 Cal, 4 g Fat, 0 g Sat Fat, 0 g Trans Fat, 0 mg Chol, 239 mg Sod, 37 g Carb, 6 g Fib, 6 g Prot, 62 mg Calc. **POINTS** value: **4.**

TRY IT Tiny bead-shaped *quinoa* (KEEN-wah) has a delicate mellow flavor similar to couscous. With the highest protein content of any grain—and its high iron content—it's a nutritional powerhouse. Find it in most supermarkets and natural-foods stores.

⅓ cup quinoa

2 teaspoons olive oil

1 onion, chopped

3 carrots, shredded

2 garlic cloves, minced

½ teaspoon ground cumin

1 cup drained rinsed canned chickpeas

½ cup orange juice

¼ cup raisins

¼ teaspoon salt

⅛ teaspoon cinnamon

1 tablespoon chopped fresh cilantro

Catch of
the Day

CHAPTER 6

**Salmon Pot-Stickers with
Sweet-and-Sour Dipping Sauce**

Salmon Pot-Stickers with Sweet-and-Sour Dipping Sauce

PREP   30 MINUTES
COOK   ABOUT 15 MINUTES
SERVES   4

1 To make the dipping sauce, combine the water, 1 tablespoon of the soy sauce, 1 tablespoon of the vinegar, one-third of the scallions, and the sugar in a small bowl; set aside.

2 To make the pot-stickers, remove and discard any skin from the salmon. With a fork, mash the salmon and any bones into tiny pieces. Stir in the carrot, the remaining scallions, the water chestnuts, ginger, and the remaining ½ teaspoon soy sauce and ½ teaspoon vinegar until blended.

3 Place the wonton skins on a clean, dry work surface. Spoon 1 teaspoon of the salmon mixture into the center of each wonton skin. Brush one-half of the edge of each wonton skin with water and fold over to seal, pressing the edges.

4 Heat 1 teaspoon of the oil in a large nonstick skillet over medium-high heat. Add 8 of the pot-stickers and cook, shaking the pan occasionally, until they are lightly browned on the bottoms, about 2 minutes. Turn over and cook about 1 minute. Add enough water to cover the pot-stickers halfway. Reduce the heat and simmer, turning the pot-stickers occasionally, until cooked through and the liquid evaporates, 4–5 minutes. Transfer to a plate and keep warm. Wipe out the skillet with a paper towel and repeat with the remaining 1 teaspoon oil and pot-stickers. Serve with the dipping sauce.

PER SERVING (4 pot-stickers with about 1 tablespoon dipping sauce): 137 Cal, 4 g Fat, 1 g Sat Fat, 0 g Trans Fat, 9 mg Chol, 522 mg Sod, 19 g Carb, 1 g Fib, 6 g Prot, 54 mg Calc. **POINTS** value: **3.**

- 2 tablespoons water
- 1 tablespoon + ½ teaspoon reduced-sodium soy sauce
- 1 tablespoon + ½ teaspoon rice vinegar
- 3 scallions, thinly sliced
- ½ teaspoon sugar
- ½ cup canned red salmon
- ¼ carrot, shredded
- 2 tablespoons chopped water chestnuts
- ½ teaspoon grated peeled fresh ginger
- 16 (3-inch) round wonton skins
- 2 teaspoons peanut oil

Pan-Seared Tuna Niçoise

PREP	15 MINUTES
COOK	ABOUT 5 MINUTES
SERVES	4

1 Combine the tomatoes, red onion, olives, basil, capers, anchovies, garlic, and oil in a bowl; set aside.

2 Sprinkle both sides of each tuna steak with the thyme, salt, and pepper.

3 Spray a large nonstick skillet with nonstick spray and set over high heat. Add the tuna and cook until browned on the outside and pink in the center, about 3 minutes on each side for medium-rare. Remove the skillet from the heat and spoon the tomato mixture over the tuna.

PER SERVING (1 tuna steak with about ½ cup tomato mixture): 247 Cal, 6 g Fat, 1 g Sat Fat, 0 g Trans Fat, 76 mg Chol, 632 mg Sod, 6 g Carb, 2 g Fib, 40 g Prot, 61 mg Calc. **POINTS** value: **5.**

HOW WE DID IT Rinsing the anchovies helps reduce the amount of salt in the recipe. Just be sure to pat them dry with a paper towel to absorb any excess water before using.

3 plum tomatoes, chopped

½ cup finely chopped red onion

¼ cup pitted and chopped kalamata olives

¼ cup coarsely chopped fresh basil

2 tablespoons capers, drained

2 anchovy fillets, rinsed, patted dry, and minced

1 garlic clove, minced

1 tablespoon extra-virgin olive oil

4 (6-ounce) tuna steaks

1 teaspoon dried thyme

½ teaspoon salt

½ teaspoon coarsely ground black pepper

Pan-Seared Tuna Niçoise

Blackened Tuna with Rémoulade Sauce

PREP 15 MINUTES
COOK ABOUT 5 MINUTES
SERVES 4

1 To make the rémoulade sauce, combine the mayonnaise, scallions, parsley, vinegar, capers, and mustard in a bowl; set aside.

2 Combine the paprika, thyme, oregano, garlic powder, cayenne, and salt in a small bowl. Sprinkle the mixture over both sides of each tuna steak.

3 Heat the oil in a large nonstick skillet over medium-high heat until just starting to smoke. Add the tuna and cook until browned on the outside and pink in the center, 2–3 minutes on each side for medium-rare. Serve the tuna with the sauce on the side.

PER SERVING (1 tuna steak with about 2 tablespoons sauce): 348 Cal, 16 g Fat, 3 g Sat Fat, 1 g Trans Fat, 79 mg Chol, 682 mg Sod, 5 g Carb, 1 g Fib, 43 g Prot, 49 mg Calc. **POINTS** value: **8.**

FOOD NOTE If you're following the **Core Plan**, use fat-free mayonnaise in the rémoulade sauce.

½ cup reduced-fat mayonnaise

2 scallions, chopped

2 tablespoons chopped fresh parsley

4 teaspoons white vinegar

2 teaspoons capers, drained and chopped

2 teaspoons whole-grain mustard

2 teaspoons paprika

1½ teaspoons dried thyme

1½ teaspoons dried oregano

1 teaspoon garlic powder

1 teaspoon cayenne

½ teaspoon salt

4 (6-ounce) tuna steaks

2 teaspoons canola oil

Seared Cod with Chunky Eggplant Sauce

PREP 10 MINUTES
COOK ABOUT 20 MINUTES
SERVES 4

1 Heat 1 teaspoon of the oil in a large nonstick skillet over medium-high heat. Add the cod and cook until browned and just opaque in the center, about 3 minutes on each side; transfer to a plate.

2 Heat the remaining 1 teaspoon oil in the skillet. Add the eggplant and water; cook, stirring occasionally, until the eggplant begins to soften and brown, about 4 minutes. Add the tomatoes, wine, olives, salt, and sugar, breaking up the tomatoes with a wooden spoon. Reduce the heat and simmer, covered, until the flavors are blended, about 10 minutes. Stir in the basil. Return the cod to the skillet; heat through.

PER SERVING (1 cod fillet with ⅓ cup sauce): 206 Cal, 5 g Fat, 1 g Sat Fat, 0 g Trans Fat, 73 mg Chol, 655 mg Sod, 8 g Carb, 2 g Fib, 32 g Prot, 65 mg Calc. ***POINTS*** value: *4.*

GOOD IDEA Serve the cod with sweet potato fries that you make yourself. Spray sweet potatoes that have been peeled and cut into ¼-inch-thick sticks with olive oil nonstick spray; spread in a single layer on a baking sheet. Bake in a preheated 450°F oven until golden, turning once, about 30 minutes.

2 teaspoons olive oil

4 (6-ounce) cod fillets

1 (½-pound) eggplant, cut into 1-inch chunks

¼ cup water

1 (14½-ounce) can peeled Italian tomatoes, with their juice

¼ cup dry white wine

10 kalamata olives, pitted and coarsely chopped

½ teaspoon salt

½ teaspoon sugar

½ cup chopped fresh basil

Lemon Cod with Spinach
and Potato Stew

Lemon Cod with Spinach and Potato Stew

PREP 15 MINUTES
COOK ABOUT 40 MINUTES
SERVES 4

1 Sprinkle both sides of the cod with the salt and pepper. Heat 1 teaspoon of the oil in a large nonstick skillet over medium-high heat. Add the cod and cook until browned and just opaque in the center, about 3 minutes on each side. Transfer to a plate and set aside.

2 Heat the remaining 2 teaspoons oil in the skillet over medium-low heat. Add the onion and garlic; cook, stirring occasionally, until the onion is very tender, about 8 minutes. Add the tomato and cook until softened, about 5 minutes. Add the potatoes, broth, lemon juice, and lemon zest; bring to a boil. Reduce the heat and simmer, covered, until the potatoes are fork-tender, about 15 minutes.

3 Meanwhile, whisk together the water and flour in a small bowl until smooth. Stir into the simmering vegetables. Add the spinach and cook, stirring constantly, until the sauce thickens and the spinach begins to wilt, 2–3 minutes. Return the cod to the skillet; heat through.

PER SERVING (1 piece cod with 1 ¼ cups stew): 282 Cal, 6 g Fat, 1 g Sat Fat, 0 g Trans Fat, 60 mg Chol, 459 mg Sod, 31 g Carb, 4 g Fib, 27 g Prot, 77 mg Calc. **POINTS** value: **5.**

HOW WE DID IT For zesting lemons, our pick is the microplane grater—available in most cookware stores. To use, hold one end of the grater over a sheet of wax paper. Stroke the lemon, in one downward motion, across the microplane's raised teeth so that just the colored zest is removed. Rotating the lemon, continue to grate so that the zest collects on the wax paper. Remove any zest still attached to the grater with a small rubber spatula.

1 pound cod fillet, cut into 4 pieces

½ teaspoon salt

¼ teaspoon freshly ground pepper

3 teaspoons olive oil

1 onion, thinly sliced

1 garlic clove, minced

1 tomato, chopped

1 pound red potatoes, scrubbed and quartered

2½ cups reduced-sodium chicken broth

1 tablespoon fresh lemon juice

2 teaspoons grated lemon zest

2 tablespoons cold water

1 tablespoon all-purpose flour

½ (10-ounce) bag fresh baby spinach, cleaned

Sesame-Crusted Swordfish with Scallion Sauce

PREP	10 MINUTES
COOK	ABOUT 10 MINUTES
SERVES	6

1 Combine the soy sauce, vinegar, honey, sesame oil, arrowroot, and crushed red pepper in a bowl; set aside.

2 Sprinkle the swordfish with the salt and ground pepper, then sprinkle with the sesame seeds, pressing the seeds onto both sides of each steak.

3 Heat the canola oil in a large nonstick skillet over medium-high heat. Add the swordfish and cook until done to taste, 2–3 minutes on each side for medium; transfer to a platter. Add the soy sauce mixture and scallions to the skillet. Bring almost to a boil and cook, stirring, until the sauce just begins to thicken, about 2 minutes. Serve the sauce with the swordfish.

PER SERVING (1 swordfish steak with about 2 tablespoons sauce): 259 Cal, 13 g Fat, 2 g Sat Fat, 0 g Trans Fat, 44 mg Chol, 570 mg Sod, 11 g Carb, 1 g Fib, 25 g Prot, 102 mg Calc. **POINTS** value: **6.**

TRY IT Arrowroot, which comes from a tropical tuber, is a thickener that can be found in the baking section of your supermarket, and turns clear when cooked. If you can't find it, substitute 1 tablespoon cornstarch.

- 3 tablespoons reduced-sodium soy sauce
- 3 tablespoons red-wine vinegar
- 2 tablespoons honey
- 1 tablespoon Asian (dark) sesame oil
- 2 teaspoons arrowroot
- ¼ teaspoon crushed red pepper
- 6 (¼-pound) swordfish steaks
- ½ teaspoon salt
- ¼ teaspoon coarsely ground black pepper
- 6 tablespoons sesame seeds
- 2 teaspoons canola oil
- 4 scallions, thinly sliced on the diagonal

Sesame-Crusted Swordfish
with Scallion Sauce

Cajun-Style Monkfish

PREP 10 MINUTES
COOK ABOUT 25 MINUTES
SERVES 4

1 Sprinkle the monkfish with 1 tablespoon of the Cajun seasoning. Heat 1 teaspoon of the oil in a large nonstick skillet over medium-high heat. Add the monkfish and cook until browned, about 3 minutes on each side. Transfer the monkfish to a plate and set aside.

2 Heat the remaining 2 teaspoons oil in the skillet over medium heat. Add the bell peppers, onion, garlic, and the remaining 1 tablespoon Cajun seasoning; cook, stirring occasionally, until the vegetables are very tender, about 8 minutes. Add the tomatoes, thyme, and sugar; bring to a boil. Return the monkfish to the skillet. Reduce the heat and simmer, covered, until the flavors are blended and the monkfish is opaque in the center, about 8 minutes.

PER SERVING (1 monkfish fillet with about ½ cup sauce): 200 Cal, 5 g Fat, 1 g Sat Fat, 0 g Trans Fat, 62 mg Chol, 1144 mg Sod, 15 g Carb, 2 g Fib, 24 g Prot, 65 mg Calc. *POINTS* value: *4.*

TRY IT Monkfish, sometimes called angler fish, is a low-fat, firm-textured fish with a mild, sweet taste.

- 1 **pound** monkfish fillets, cut into 4 pieces
- 2 **tablespoons** Cajun seasoning
- 3 **teaspoons** olive oil
- 2 **green bell peppers,** seeded and sliced
- 1 **large** onion, sliced
- 2 **garlic cloves,** minced
- 1 **(14½-ounce) can** stewed tomatoes
- 1 **tablespoon chopped** fresh thyme, or 1 teaspoon dried
- 1 **teaspoon** sugar

Cornmeal-and-Almond Trout

PREP 5 MINUTES
COOK ABOUT 15 MINUTES
SERVES 2

1 Combine the cornmeal, almonds, 1/4 teaspoon of the salt, and 1/8 teaspoon of the pepper in a food processor or blender and grind to a fine consistency. Transfer to a large, flat plate or a sheet of wax paper. Spray the trout with olive oil nonstick spray and season with salt and pepper, including the cavities of each fish. Roll in the nut mixture to coat all over.

2 Melt the butter in a large nonstick skillet over medium heat. Add the trout and cook until browned, about 5 minutes on each side. Reduce the heat to low and cook, covered, until the trout is just opaque in the center, 2–3 minutes on each side. Serve with the lemon wedges.

PER SERVING (1 trout): 139 Cal, 8 g Fat, 2 g Sat Fat, 0 g Trans Fat, 33 mg Chol, 309 mg Sod, 7 g Carb, 1 g Fib, 10 g Prot, 42 mg Calc. *POINTS* value: *3.*

FOOD NOTE Readily available and often inexpensive farm-raised rainbow trout are larger and sweeter than brook trout. If you'd like to prepare for more than two servings, cook the trout in batches or use multiple skillets.

2 **tablespoons** cornmeal

1 **tablespoon sliced** almonds

1/4 **teaspoon** salt + additional to season fish

1/8 **teaspoon coarsely** ground black pepper + additional to season fish

2 (3/4-pound) **whole** rainbow trout, cleaned

1/2 **tablespoon** butter

4 lemon wedges

Citrus Red Snapper

PREP 15 MINUTES
COOK ABOUT 10 MINUTES
SERVES 4

1 Combine the flour, coriander, ginger, and cayenne on a sheet of wax paper. Coat one side of each fillet with the flour mixture.

2 Heat the oil in a large nonstick skillet over medium-high heat. Add the fillets, floured-side down, and cook until browned on the bottoms, 2–3 minutes. Transfer to a plate.

3 Add the bell pepper, scallions, broth, orange juice, lemon juice, and lime juice to the skillet; return the fillets to the skillet, browned-side up. Reduce the heat and cook, covered, until the fillets are just opaque in the center and the bell pepper is softened, 3–5 minutes. With a slotted spatula, transfer the fillets and vegetables to a platter. Cook the pan juices until they are reduced to about ¼ cup, about 3 minutes; pour over the fillets. Serve, garnished with the lemon and lime slices.

PER SERVING (1 snapper fillet with about ¼ cup vegetables and 1 tablespoon sauce): 279 Cal, 5 g Fat, 1 g Sat Fat, 0 g Trans Fat, 84 mg Chol, 150 mg Sod, 7 g Carb, 1 g Fib, 48 g Prot, 83 mg Calc. **POINTS** value: *6.*

FOOD NOTE Just about any firm-flesh fish fillets will do the trick in this zesty recipe. Try ocean perch, flounder, sea bass, cod, haddock, or whatever looks best at the fish counter.

2 **tablespoons all-purpose flour**

¾ **teaspoon ground coriander**

¾ **teaspoon ground ginger**

¼ **teaspoon** cayenne

4 **(½-pound) red snapper fillets**

2 **teaspoons vegetable oil**

1 **yellow bell pepper, seeded and sliced**

3 **scallions,** sliced

¼ **cup reduced-sodium chicken broth**

2 **tablespoons orange juice**

1 **tablespoon fresh lemon juice**

1 **tablespoon fresh lime juice**

Lemon and lime slices, for garnish

Sesame-Glazed Shrimp with Snow Peas and Baby Corn

PREP 20 MINUTES
COOK ABOUT 10 MINUTES
SERVES 4

1 Whisk together the hoisin sauce, soy sauce, sherry, honey, and cornstarch in a bowl until smooth; set aside.

2 Heat a large nonstick skillet or wok over high heat until a drop of water sizzles. Add 2 teaspoons of the sesame oil, swirl to coat the pan, then add the shrimp. Stir-fry until just opaque in the center, 3–4 minutes; transfer to a bowl.

3 Add the remaining 1 teaspoon sesame oil to the skillet, swirl to coat the pan, then add the ginger, garlic, and scallions. Stir-fry until fragrant, about 30 seconds. Add the snow peas and baby corn; stir-fry until the snow peas are bright green, about 3 minutes. Stir in the hoisin mixture and the shrimp. Bring to a boil and cook, stirring, until thickened, 1–2 minutes. Remove the skillet from the heat and stir in the sesame seeds.

PER SERVING (1¼ cups): 286 Cal, 7 g Fat, 1 g Sat Fat, 0 g Trans Fat, 210 mg Chol, 763 mg Sod, 21 g Carb, 5 g Fib, 32 g Prot, 127 mg Calc. **POINTS** value: *6.*

FOOD NOTE If you prefer, you can substitute an equal amount of water for the sherry.

2 tablespoons hoisin sauce

2 tablespoons reduced-sodium soy sauce

2 tablespoons sherry

1 tablespoon honey

2 teaspoons cornstarch

3 teaspoons Asian (dark) sesame oil

1½ pounds large shrimp, peeled and deveined

1 tablespoon grated peeled fresh ginger

1 garlic clove, minced

2 large scallions, chopped

½ pound fresh snow peas, trimmed

1 (8-ounce) can baby corn, drained

2 teaspoons sesame seeds

Corn, Tomato, and Shrimp Sauté

Corn, Tomato, and Shrimp Sauté

PREP 10 MINUTES
COOK ABOUT 10 MINUTES
SERVES 4

1 Heat 2 tablespoons of the oil in a large nonstick skillet over medium-high heat. Add the shrimp and cook until lightly golden, about 1 minute on each side. Transfer the shrimp to a plate.

2 Heat the remaining ½ tablespoon oil in the skillet. Add the onion and garlic; cook, stirring frequently, until the onion begins to soften, about 1 minute. Stir in the corn and cook until crisp-tender, about 1 minute. Add the tomatoes and cook about 1 minute. Add the shrimp and cook, stirring frequently, until heated through, 1–2 minutes. Remove the skillet from the heat and stir in the basil, salt, and pepper.

PER SERVING (1 cup): 290 Cal, 12 g Fat, 2 g Sat Fat, 0 g Trans Fat, 172 mg Chol, 471 mg Sod, 23 g Carb, 3 g Fib, 26 g Prot, 80 mg Calc. **POINTS** value: **6.**

EXPRESS LANE To save time, consider purchasing precleaned (but not precooked) frozen shrimp at your fish market. Either thaw the shrimp overnight in the refrigerator, or run under cold water until thawed, 4 to 5 minutes. In a pinch, frozen corn can also be substituted for the fresh.

2½ tablespoons olive oil

1 pound peeled and deveined medium shrimp

½ cup chopped onion

2 garlic cloves, minced

1½ cups fresh corn kernels (from 2 corn-on-the-cobs)

2 cups cherry tomatoes

½ cup chopped fresh basil

¼ teaspoon salt

¼ teaspoon coarsely ground black pepper

Garlicky Shrimp Scampi

PREP 20 MINUTES
COOK ABOUT 10 MINUTES
SERVES 4

1 Preheat the broiler.

2 Heat the oil in a large nonstick skillet with an ovenproof handle over medium-high heat. Add the shrimp, garlic, salt, and pepper; cook, stirring frequently, just until the shrimp begin to turn pink, about 3 minutes. Add the wine, broth, scallions, parsley, and lemon juice; bring to a boil. Reduce the heat and simmer, uncovered, until the liquid begins to thicken slightly and the shrimp are just opaque in the center, about 3 minutes.

3 Top the shrimp mixture with the bread crumbs. Place the skillet under the broiler and broil 5 inches from the heat until the topping is golden, about 2 minutes.

PER SERVING (1¼ cups): 137 Cal, 5 g Fat, 1 g Sat Fat, 0 g Trans Fat, 107 mg Chol, 359 mg Sod, 9 g Carb, 1 g Fib, 13 g Prot, 61 mg Calc. *POINTS* value: *3.*

HOW WE DID IT To butterfly shrimp, peel the shrimp. Then, using a paring knife, slice along the back of the shrimp from top to tail, cutting the shrimp almost but not entirely in half. With the blade of your knife, scrape out the vein and flatten the shrimp slightly.

1 **tablespoon** olive oil

1 **pound** large shrimp, peeled, deveined, and butterflied

3 **garlic cloves,** minced

¼ **teaspoon** salt

¼ **teaspoon freshly ground pepper**

½ **cup** dry white wine

½ **cup** reduced-sodium chicken broth

3 **scallions,** sliced

2 **tablespoons chopped fresh parsley**

2 **tablespoons** fresh lemon juice

⅓ **cup** plain dry bread crumbs

Garlicky Shrimp Scampi

Shrimp in Lime Butter Sauce

PREP 20 MINUTES
COOK ABOUT 10 MINUTES
SERVES 4

1 Make a cut along the outer curved side of each shrimp. Hold under cold running water to rinse out the veins. Pat them dry with paper towels, then spray the shrimp with olive oil nonstick spray.

2 Heat a large nonstick skillet over medium heat. Add the shrimp and cook until just opaque in the center, 3–4 minutes on each side. Transfer the shrimp to a plate.

3 Add the broth and garlic to the skillet; cook until the broth is reduced by one-half, 3–4 minutes. Stir in the lime juice and cook about 30 seconds. Add the shrimp and butter, stirring to blend. Stir in the cilantro and cook until the shrimp is heated through, about 30 seconds. Season with salt and pepper.

PER SERVING (about 5 shrimp with about 2 tablespoons sauce): 163 Cal, 6 g Fat, 2 g Sat Fat, 0 g Trans Fat, 181 mg Chol, 420 mg Sod, 3 g Carb, 0 g Fib, 24 g Prot, 68 mg Calc. *POINTS* value: *4.*

HOW WE DID IT Sautéing shrimp in their shells eliminates the need to use a lot of oil to keep them from sticking to the pan and also makes for a stunning presentation. Use scissors or a small paring knife to cut the shells; this facilitates cleaning the shrimp and makes them easier to peel.

1 **pound large shrimp**

1 cup **chicken broth**

4 **garlic cloves**, minced

2 tablespoons **fresh lime juice**

1 tablespoon **butter**

¼ cup chopped **fresh cilantro**

Salt to taste

Coarsely ground black **pepper** to taste

Sea Scallop Salad

PREP 15 MINUTES
COOK ABOUT 5 MINUTES
SERVES 4

1 Sprinkle the scallops with ½ teaspoon of the salt and the pepper. Spray a large nonstick skillet with nonstick spray and set over medium-high heat. Add the scallops and cook, stirring occasionally, until browned, 3–4 minutes.

2 Meanwhile, whisk together the orange juice, oil, lemon juice, honey, and the remaining ¼ teaspoon salt in a large bowl. Add the oranges, grapefruit, red onion, and olives. Stir in the scallops.

3 Divide the mesclun among 4 plates; top each with an equal amount of the scallop salad. Sprinkle with the mint (if using).

PER SERVING (about 2 cups): 251 Cal, 9 g Fat, 1 g Sat Fat, 0 g Trans Fat, 37 mg Chol, 677 mg Sod, 23 g Carb, 4 g Fib, 21 g Prot, 99 mg Calc. *POINTS* value: **5.**

HOW WE DID IT Thoroughly pat the scallops dry with paper towels before you sauté them, and arrange in a single layer in the skillet, making sure they don't touch each other; otherwise, they will steam instead of brown.

1 **pound** sea scallops

¾ **teaspoon** salt

½ **teaspoon coarsely ground black pepper**

¼ **cup** orange juice

2 **tablespoons** olive oil

1 **tablespoon fresh lemon juice**

1 **teaspoon** honey

2 **navel oranges, peeled and coarsely chopped**

1 **ruby red grapefruit, peeled and coarsely chopped**

½ **cup thinly sliced red onion**

6 **oil-cured black olives, pitted**

4 **cups mesclun salad greens**

2 **tablespoons chopped fresh mint** (optional)

Scallops with Salsa Cruda

PREP 15 MINUTES
COOK ABOUT 25 MINUTES
SERVES 6

1 To make the salsa, combine the tomatoes, basil, parsley, onion, 2½ tablespoons of the oil, the vinegar, garlic, ½ teaspoon of the salt, and ¼ teaspoon of the pepper in a large bowl.

2 Meanwhile, cook the pasta according to package directions omitting the salt, if desired; drain. Add the pasta to the bowl with the salsa; toss to coat.

3 Sprinkle the scallops with the remaining ¼ teaspoon salt and ¼ teaspoon pepper. Heat the remaining ½ tablespoon oil in a large nonstick skillet over medium-high heat. Add the scallops and cook, shaking the skillet occasionally, until lightly browned and just opaque in the center, 3–5 minutes. Transfer to the bowl with the pasta mixture and mix well.

PER SERVING (about 1 cup): 298 Cal, 9 g Fat, 1 g Sat Fat, 0 g Trans Fat, 25 mg Chol, 477 mg Sod, 37 g Carb, 3 g Fib, 19 g Prot, 45 mg Calc. *POINTS* value: *6.*

FOOD NOTE When bay scallops are in season in the fall, they're unbeatable for flavor; otherwise, use quartered sea scallops.

1½ **pounds** ripe tomatoes, **seeded and chopped**

½ **cup chopped fresh basil**

½ **cup chopped fresh parsley**

½ **cup chopped** onion

3 **tablespoons** extra-virgin olive oil

2 **tablespoons** balsamic vinegar

1 **garlic clove, minced**

¾ **teaspoon** salt

½ **teaspoon coarsely ground black pepper**

½ **(1-pound) box medium pasta shells**

1 **pound** bay scallops

Seared Scallops on Scallion Orzo

PREP 10 MINUTES
COOK ABOUT 25 MINUTES
SERVES 4

1 Cook the orzo according to package directions omitting the salt, if desired; drain.

2 Meanwhile, heat 1½ tablespoons of the oil in a large nonstick skillet over medium-high heat. Add the garlic and cook, stirring constantly, until fragrant, about 1 minute. Stir in the bell pepper and cook until crisp-tender, about 2 minutes. Add the scallions and cook, stirring constantly, until wilted, about 30 seconds.

3 Remove the skillet from the heat and add the orzo, lemon juice, and ½ teaspoon of the salt; keep warm.

4 Sprinkle the scallops with the remaining ½ teaspoon salt and the ground pepper. Heat the remaining ½ tablespoon oil in another large nonstick skillet over medium-high heat. Add the scallops and cook until lightly browned and just opaque in the center, 1–2 minutes on each side. Serve over the orzo.

PER SERVING (1⅓ cups scallops with ¾ cup orzo): 342 Cal, 8 g Fat, 1 g Sat Fat, 0 g Trans Fat, 37 mg Chol, 845 mg Sod, 41 g Carb, 3 g Fib, 26 g Prot, 64 mg Calc. *POINTS* value: **7.**

1 cup orzo

2 tablespoons olive oil

2 garlic cloves, sliced

1 red bell pepper, seeded and finely chopped

1 cup chopped scallions (8–10 scallions)

2 tablespoons fresh lemon juice

1 teaspoon salt

1 pound sea scallops

½ teaspoon coarsely ground black pepper

PLAY IT SAFE When purchasing scallops, look for a moist sheen and a fresh, sweet scent. Refrigerate as soon as you bring them home, and use within 2 days.

Scallop-Cucumber Stir-Fry

Scallop-Cucumber Stir-Fry

PREP	15 MINUTES PLUS 30 MINUTES MARINATING AND STANDING TIME
COOK	ABOUT 15 MINUTES
SERVES	4

1 Combine the wine, ginger, and onion powder in a zip-close plastic bag; add the scallops. Squeeze out the air and seal the bag; turn to coat the scallops. Refrigerate, turning the bag occasionally, at least 30 minutes. Drain the scallops, reserving the marinade. Pat the scallops dry with a paper towel.

2 Meanwhile, layer the cucumber slices in a colander, sprinkling with the salt between each layer. Let stand in the sink about 20 minutes to drain, then rinse and pat the slices dry with a paper towel.

3 Whisk together the broth, cornstarch, sesame oil, and sugar in a small bowl until smooth; set aside.

4 Heat a large nonstick skillet or wok over high heat until a drop of water sizzles. Add 1 teaspoon of the peanut oil, swirl to coat the pan, then add the scallops. Stir-fry until just opaque in the center, 1–2 minutes. Transfer to a plate and keep warm.

5 Heat the remaining 1 teaspoon peanut oil in the skillet. Add the cucumbers, carrots, and the marinade; bring to a boil. Reduce the heat and cook, tossing lightly, until the cucumbers are crisp-tender, about 2 minutes. Add the scallops and the broth mixture; cook, stirring, until the sauce thickens, 1–2 minutes.

PER SERVING (about 1 cup): 209 Cal, 5 g Fat, 1 g Sat Fat, 0 g Trans Fat, 47 mg Chol, 533 mg Sod, 14 g Carb, 2 g Fib, 25 g Prot, 68 mg Calc. **POINTS** value: **4.**

HOW WE DID IT Be sure to pull off and discard the tough crescent-shaped muscle attached to any of the scallops before marinating in step 1.

2 tablespoons rice wine or dry sherry

½ teaspoon minced peeled fresh ginger

¼ teaspoon onion powder

1¼ pounds sea scallops

4 cucumbers, peeled, halved lengthwise, seeded, and sliced

1 teaspoon salt

¼ cup reduced-sodium chicken broth

2 teaspoons cornstarch

1 teaspoon Asian (dark) sesame oil

½ teaspoon sugar

2 teaspoons peanut oil

2 carrots, diced and steamed

Paella

PREP	25 MINUTES
COOK	ABOUT 30 MINUTES
SERVES	4

1 Heat the oil in a large nonstick skillet over medium-high heat. Add the bell pepper, scallions, and garlic; cook, stirring frequently, until softened, about 5 minutes. Add the rice and cook, stirring constantly, until coated, about 1 minute.

2 Stir in the broth and saffron; bring to a boil. Reduce the heat and simmer, covered, about 10 minutes. Stir in the tomatoes, cod, mussels, shrimp, sausage, peas, wine, parsley, bay leaf, lemon juice, salt, and pepper; simmer, stirring occasionally, until the rice is tender and the seafood is cooked through, 10–15 minutes. Discard the garlic, bay leaf, and any unopened mussels. Serve at once.

PER SERVING (about 2 cups): 412 Cal, 10 g Fat, 2 g Sat Fat, 0 g Trans Fat, 90 mg Chol, 725 mg Sod, 49 g Carb, 3 g Fib, 28 g Prot, 69 mg Calc. *POINTS* value: *8.*

HOW WE DID IT The hairy filaments that protrude from a mussel are known as a "beard." To remove, pinch the filaments between the thumb and forefinger and pull firmly. Some mussels available today have no beards.

2 tablespoons olive oil

1 bell pepper, chopped

4 scallions, thinly sliced

4 garlic cloves, crushed

2 cups white rice

3 cups reduced-sodium chicken broth

Pinch saffron threads

1 (14½-ounce) can stewed tomatoes

¾ pound cod, cut into chunks

½ pound mussels, scrubbed

½ pound medium shrimp, peeled and deveined

4 Italian turkey sausage links, cooked and sliced

1 cup thawed frozen peas

½ cup dry white wine

2 tablespoons chopped fresh parsley

1 bay leaf

1 tablespoon fresh lemon juice

½ teaspoon salt

¼ teaspoon pepper

Paella

Get Your
Veggies

CHAPTER 7

Potato-Zucchini Pancakes

PREP 15 MINUTES PLUS 10 MINUTES STANDING TIME
COOK ABOUT 25 MINUTES
SERVES 4

1 Toss the potatoes, zucchini, and salt in a medium bowl; let stand 10 minutes. Squeeze out the liquid and discard. Stir the egg, scallions, flour, tarragon, and pepper into the potato mixture.

2 Heat ¼ teaspoon of the oil in a large nonstick skillet over medium heat. Drop the potato mixture, 2 tablespoons at a time, into mounds and flatten with a spatula; cook until the bottoms are lightly browned, about 6 minutes. Turn the pancakes over, add ¼ teaspoon of the oil, and cook until lightly browned and cooked through, about 6 minutes. Repeat with the remaining oil and potato mixture to make 8 pancakes. Serve with the sour cream (if using).

PER SERVING (2 pancakes with 1 teaspoon sour cream): 155 Cal, 3 g Fat, 1 g Sat Fat, 0 g Trans Fat, 55 mg Chol, 610 mg Sod, 27 g Carb, 3 g Fib, 6 g Prot, 38 mg Calc. *POINTS* value: *3.*

FOOD NOTE If you only have one large zucchini, cut out the seeds before shredding it. They add a bitter flavor and unpleasant texture (smaller zucchini have smaller seeds, so the flavor and texture are less obtrusive).

2 large **russet potatoes,** peeled and shredded (about 2 cups)

2 medium **zucchini,** shredded (2 cups)

1 teaspoon **salt**

1 large **egg**

3 **scallions,** sliced

2 tablespoons **all-purpose flour**

½ teaspoon **dried tarragon,** crumbled

⅛ teaspoon **freshly ground pepper**

1 teaspoon **olive oil**

4 teaspoons **light sour cream** (optional)

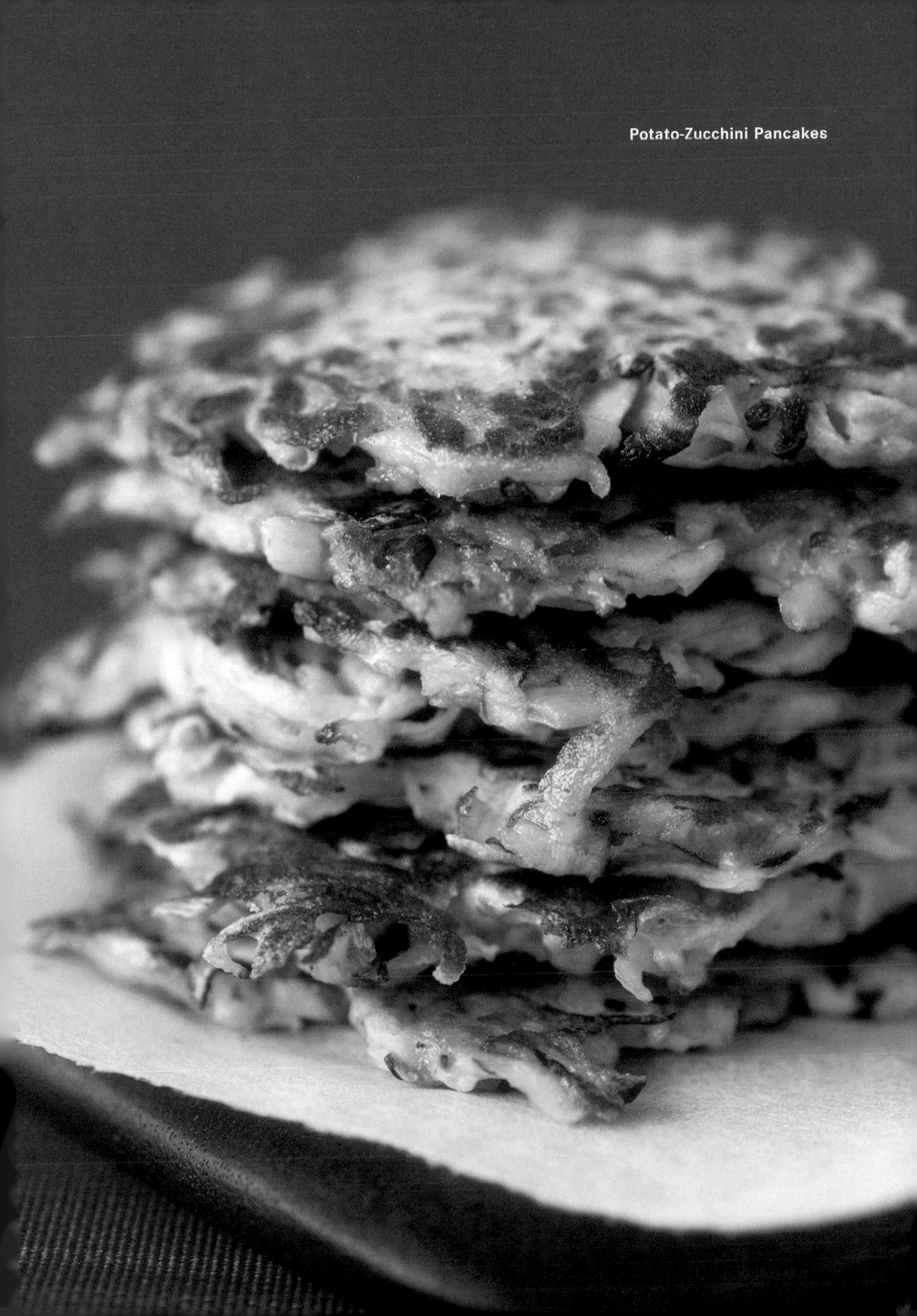
Potato-Zucchini Pancakes

Vegetarian Fajitas

PREP 15 MINUTES
COOK ABOUT 20 MINUTES
SERVES 4

1 Heat the oil in a large nonstick skillet over medium heat. Add the bell peppers, onions, zucchini, squash, jalapeños, garlic, salt, and ground pepper; cook, stirring frequently, until the vegetables are very soft, about 20 minutes.

2 Meanwhile, heat the refried beans according to package directions.

3 Place the vegetables, beans, lettuce, salsa, and sour cream in separate bowls; arrange on the serving table. Place 2 tortillas on each of 4 plates and serve, allowing each person to fill and roll their own fajitas.

PER SERVING (2 fajitas): 459 Cal, 10 g Fat, 1 g Sat Fat, 1 g Trans Fat, 0 mg Chol, 1177 mg Sod, 78 g Carb, 9 g Fib, 16 g Prot, 202 mg Calc. **POINTS** value: **9.**

EXPRESS LANE For a jumpstart on dinner, make the vegetables a day ahead, and reheat them just before serving the fajitas.

4 teaspoons olive oil

2 green bell peppers, seeded and cut into strips

2 onions, thinly sliced

1 zucchini, sliced

1 medium yellow squash, sliced

2 jalapeño peppers, seeded and minced (wear gloves to prevent irritation)

4 garlic cloves, minced

½ teaspoon salt

¼ teaspoon freshly ground pepper

1 (16-ounce) can fat-free refried beans

4 cups finely shredded iceberg lettuce

½ cup fat-free salsa

½ cup fat-free sour cream

8 (6-inch) flour tortillas

Black Bean Tostadas

PREP	10 MINUTES
COOK	ABOUT 20 MINUTES
SERVES	4

1 Preheat the oven to 350°F. Place the tortillas on a baking sheet; bake, turning frequently, until golden and crisp, about 8 minutes.

2 Meanwhile, heat the oil in a large nonstick skillet over medium-high heat. Add the onion and cook, stirring frequently, until softened, about 5 minutes. Add the beans, tomato, currants, vinegar, garlic, and chili powder; cook, mashing the beans with the back of a wooden spoon, until heated through, about 10 minutes.

3 Spread the bean mixture over the tortillas; layer each with one-quarter of the lettuce, avocado, salsa, and sour cream.

PER SERVING (1 tostada): 258 Cal, 8 g Fat, 0 g Sat Fat, 0 g Trans Fat, 0 mg Chol, 344 mg Sod, 40 g Carb, 13 g Fib, 10 g Prot, 118 mg Calc. **POINTS** value: *5.*

EXPRESS LANE Make and refrigerate the bean mixture in an airtight container a day or two ahead—it not only gives the flavors time to blend, but it also simplifies getting dinner on the table.

4 (6-inch) flour tortillas

2 teaspoons vegetable oil

1 onion, chopped

1 (19-ounce) can black beans, rinsed and drained

1 tomato, diced

1 tablespoon currants

1 tablespoon red-wine vinegar

2 garlic cloves, minced

1 teaspoon chili powder

2 cups shredded iceberg lettuce

½ medium avocado, peeled and diced

¼ cup salsa

¼ cup fat-free sour cream

Spinach Omelette

PREP 10 MINUTES PLUS 5 MINUTES COOLING TIME
COOK ABOUT 5 MINUTES
SERVES 1

1 In a medium saucepan, cook the spinach with the water that clings to its leaves until just wilted, about 2 minutes. Drain well, squeezing out all the liquid. Cool slightly, then chop finely.

2 Meanwhile, whisk together the eggs, water, cheese, salt, and pepper in a medium bowl.

3 Heat the oil in a small nonstick skillet until a drop of water sizzles. Pour in the egg mixture and swirl to cover the pan. Reduce the heat and cook until the underside is set and the top is still a little creamy, about 2 minutes. Sprinkle the spinach evenly over half of the omelette; fold the other half over the filling and cook until the eggs are completely set, about 1 minute. Slide the omelette onto a plate.

PER SERVING: 216 Cal, 14 g Fat, 4 g Sat Fat, 0 g Trans Fat, 427 mg Chol, 880 mg Sod, 7 g Carb, 4 g Fib, 18 g Prot, 236 mg Calc. **POINTS** value: **5.**

GOOD IDEA If you like a zestier omelette, add ¼ cup chopped tomato and a few drops hot pepper sauce to the mixture just before folding the omelette (the per-serving **POINTS** value will remain the same).

2½ cups coarsely chopped cleaned spinach (do not dry)

2 large eggs

1 tablespoon water

2 teaspoons grated Parmesan cheese

½ teaspoon salt

¼ teaspoon freshly ground pepper

½ teaspoon olive oil

Sautéed Swiss Chard and Chickpeas

PREP	10 MINUTES
COOK	ABOUT 10 MINUTES
SERVES	4

1 Heat the oil and butter in a large nonstick saucepan, stirring constantly, over medium-high heat, until the butter melts and the bubbling nearly subsides. Add the cumin and cook, stirring constantly, until just fragrant, 10–15 seconds. Add the chiles (if using) and garlic; cook, stirring constantly, until the garlic is lightly browned, 30–45 seconds.

2 Immediately add the chard stems, the chickpeas, and ¼ cup of the water; cook, stirring gently, until the stems are softened and most of the liquid evaporates, 3–4 minutes. Stir in the chard leaves, the ginger, and the remaining ¼ cup water. Reduce the heat and simmer, stirring occasionally, until chard is just tender, 4–5 minutes. Sprinkle with the garam masala and cook, uncovered, stirring gently, until the remaining liquid is absorbed, 1–2 minutes.

PER SERVING (about 1 cup): 166 Cal, 6 g Fat, 2 g Sat Fat, 0 g Trans Fat, 5 mg Chol, 157 mg Sod, 20 g Carb, 7 g Fib, 8 g Prot, 97 mg Calc. *POINTS* value: *3.*

TRY IT *Garam masala* (gah-RAHM mah-SAH-lah), a blend of dry-roasted ground spices from India, is now available in many supermarkets. If you can't find it, combine ½ teaspoon ground cardamom, ¼ teaspoon ground coriander, and a pinch each of cinnamon and freshly ground pepper.

2 teaspoons corn oil

2 teaspoons unsalted butter

½ teaspoon ground cumin

1 tablespoon canned chopped green chiles (optional)

1 garlic clove, minced

1 bunch Swiss chard, cleaned and chopped (separate the stems and leaves)

1 (19-ounce) can chickpeas, rinsed and drained

½ cup water

½ teaspoon ground ginger

¾ teaspoon garam masala

Asian Barley Sauté

Asian Barley Sauté

PREP 15 MINUTES
COOK ABOUT 50 MINUTES
SERVES 4

1 Cook the barley according to package directions.

2 Meanwhile, heat the oil in a large nonstick skillet over medium-high heat. Add the mushrooms and cook, stirring occasionally, until golden, 5–6 minutes.

3 Add the barley, snow peas, scallions, and ginger; cook, stirring frequently, until the snow peas are bright green, 1–2 minutes. Stir in the water chestnuts, orange juice, and soy sauce; cook, stirring occasionally, until the liquid is absorbed, about 5 minutes. Stir in the orange zest.

PER SERVING (about 1 ½ cups): 244 Cal, 4 g Fat, 1 g Sat Fat, 0 g Trans Fat, 0 mg Chol, 323 mg Sod, 49 g Carb, 8 g Fib, 6 g Prot, 53 mg Calc. *POINTS* value: *4.*

EXPRESS LANE To save time, cook the barley ahead and store it in the refrigerator up to 2 days, then proceed with the recipe as directed.

½ cup pearl barley

1 tablespoon vegetable oil

½ pound fresh shiitake mushrooms, stems discarded and diced

2 cups trimmed fresh snow peas, sliced

8 scallions, thinly sliced

1 tablespoon grated peeled fresh ginger

2 (8-ounce) cans sliced water chestnuts, drained

½ cup orange juice

2 tablespoons reduced-sodium soy sauce

½ teaspoon grated orange zest

Braised Fresh Fava Beans

PREP 20 MINUTES
COOK ABOUT 35 MINUTES
SERVES 4

1 Remove the beans from the pods; you should have about 2 cups beans. Bring a large pot of lightly salted water to a boil. Add the beans and cook just until they turn bright green, about 30 seconds. Drain, rinsing under cold water; remove the skins.

2 Heat the oil in a large nonstick skillet over medium-high heat. Add the onion and cook, stirring frequently, until softened, about 5 minutes. Add the beans, wine, garlic, thyme, salt, and pepper; cook, covered, until the beans are tender, about 10 minutes. Stir in the lemon juice and serve at once.

PER SERVING (about ½ cup): 161 Cal, 3 g Fat, 0 g Sat Fat, 0 g Trans Fat, 0 mg Chol, 308 mg Sod, 24 g Carb, 5 g Fib, 6 g Prot, 44 mg Calc. **POINTS** value: **3.**

FOOD NOTE Peak season for fresh fava beans is April through June. Choose pods that are not bulging with beans—the bulges mean that the beans are older and tougher. If you cannot find fresh favas, substitute large fresh lima beans and skip step 1.

2 **pounds fresh fava bean pods**

2 **teaspoons olive oil**

1 **onion, chopped**

½ **cup dry white wine**

2 **garlic cloves, minced**

½ **teaspoon dried thyme**

½ **teaspoon salt**

¼ **teaspoon freshly ground pepper**

1 **tablespoon fresh lemon juice**

Sweet-and-Sour Cabbage with Peanuts

PREP 15 MINUTES
COOK ABOUT 15 MINUTES
SERVES 4

1 Spray a large nonstick skillet with nonstick spray and set over medium-high heat. Add the onion and cook, stirring frequently, until softened, about 5 minutes.

2 Add the cabbage, carrots, and water; cook, stirring occasionally, until the carrots are softened, 5–6 minutes. Stir in the tomatoes, vinegar, sugar, salt, and pepper; cook, stirring occasionally, until heated through, 2–3 minutes. Sprinkle with the peanuts; serve topped with the yogurt.

PER SERVING (about 1½ cups): 214 Cal, 10 g Fat, 1 g Sat Fat, 0 g Trans Fat, 1 mg Chol, 374 mg Sod, 26 g Carb, 6 g Fib, 10 g Prot, 202 mg Calc. *POINTS* value: *4.*

GOOD IDEA This hearty dish is perfect over white rice or potatoes (½ cup cooked rice or 1 cup cooked potatoes for each serving will increase the *POINTS* value by 2).

1 **onion, chopped**

1 small **green cabbage,** chopped

2 **carrots, thinly sliced**

½ cup **water**

½ cup canned **crushed tomatoes (no salt added)**

¼ cup **red-wine vinegar**

1 tablespoon **sugar**

½ teaspoon **salt**

Freshly **ground pepper** to taste

½ cup unsalted **dry-roasted peanuts,** chopped

1 cup **plain fat-free yogurt**

Sautéed Red Cabbage and Apples

PREP   15 MINUTES
COOK   ABOUT 20 MINUTES
SERVES   4

Heat the oil in a large nonstick skillet over medium-high heat. Add the onion and cook, stirring frequently, until softened, about 5 minutes. Stir in the cabbage, water, honey, and caraway seeds. Reduce the heat and simmer, covered, until the cabbage is barely tender, about 8 minutes. Add the apple, vinegar, salt, and pepper. Cook, covered, until the cabbage is very tender, about 6 minutes.

PER SERVING (about 1 cup): 80 Cal, 2 g Fat, 0 g Sat Fat, 0 g Trans Fat, 0 mg Chol, 308 mg Sod, 17 g Carb, 3 g Fib, 2 g Prot, 53 mg Calc. **POINTS** value: **1.**

GOOD IDEA This colorful dish is a natural with pork (a 2-ounce broiled pork chop for each serving will increase the **POINTS** value by 4).

1 teaspoon olive oil

1 onion, sliced

½ small red cabbage, sliced (about 5 cups)

½ cup water

1 tablespoon honey

½ teaspoon caraway seeds

1 Golden Delicious apple, peeled and diced

2 tablespoons red-wine vinegar

½ teaspoon salt

¼ teaspoon freshly ground pepper

Sautéed Red Cabbage
and Apples

Clockwise from top: Broccoli in Oyster Sauce, page 37, Dry-Cooked Green Beans, page 185, and Hot-and-Sour Cabbage

Hot-and-Sour Cabbage

PREP	15 MINUTES
COOK	ABOUT 15 MINUTES
SERVES	4

1 Whisk together the vinegar, soy sauce, cornstarch, and sugar in a small bowl until smooth; set aside.

2 Heat a large nonstick skillet or wok over high heat until a drop of water sizzles. Add 2 teaspoons of the peanut oil, swirl to coat the pan, then add the white cabbage chunks. Stir-fry until the pieces are thoroughly coated with the oil, about 1 minute. Add the water and cook about 1 minute. Stir in the green cabbage chunks and stir-fry until crisp-tender, about 2 minutes. Transfer to a medium bowl and toss with the sesame oil.

3 Add the remaining 1 teaspoon peanut oil to the skillet, swirl to coat the pan, then add the chile peppers. Stir-fry until blackened, about 1 minute. Add the scallions and ginger; stir-fry until the scallions are softened, 3–4 minutes. Add the chili paste and cook about 5 seconds; add the cabbage and stir-fry about 2 minutes. Stir in the vinegar mixture and cook, tossing lightly, until the sauce thickens and coats the cabbage, 2–3 minutes.

PER SERVING (about 1 cup): 77 Cal, 5 g Fat, 1 g Sat Fat, 0 g Trans Fat, 0 mg Chol, 179 mg Sod, 8 g Carb, 1 g Fib, 2 g Prot, 96 mg Calc. *POINTS* value: *2.*

2 tablespoons white vinegar

1 tablespoon reduced-sodium soy sauce

2 teaspoons cornstarch

1 teaspoon sugar

3 teaspoons peanut oil

6 cups chopped napa cabbage (1-inch chunks), green and white parts separated

¼ cup water

1 teaspoon Asian (dark) sesame oil

3-4 dried Szechuan chile peppers, seeds removed and discarded

4 scallions, thinly sliced

1 (½-inch) piece peeled fresh ginger, minced

½ teaspoon hot chili paste

TRY IT Unlike regular green cabbage, napa cabbage, also known as Chinese cabbage, features thin, crisp leaves that are delicately mild. Choose firm, tightly packed heads with crisp, green-tipped leaves. Refrigerate, tightly wrapped, up to 3 days.

Braised Cabbage

PREP 10 MINUTES
COOK ABOUT 30 MINUTES
SERVES 4

Heat the oil in a large nonstick skillet over medium-high heat. Add the onion and cook, stirring frequently, until softened, about 5 minutes. Stir in the cabbage, apple juice, vinegar, sugar, salt, and bay leaf; cook, covered, until the cabbage is very tender, about 20 minutes. Discard the bay leaf and stir in the apple; cook, uncovered, until the apple is tender, about 5 minutes.

PER SERVING (about ½ cup): 97 Cal, 3 g Fat, 0 g Sat Fat, 0 g Trans Fat, 0 mg Chol, 156 mg Sod, 19 g Carb, 3 g Fib, 2 g Prot, 52 mg Calc. **POINTS** value: **2.**

FOOD NOTE Although we like this dish with red cabbage, you can use green if you prefer.

- 2 teaspoons vegetable oil
- 1 onion, thinly sliced
- ½ medium red cabbage, very thinly sliced
- ½ cup apple juice
- 1 tablespoon apple-cider vinegar
- 2 teaspoons sugar
- ¼ teaspoon salt
- 1 bay leaf
- 1 Granny Smith apple, shredded

Cumin-Scented Carrots and Sugar-Snap Peas

PREP 10 MINUTES
COOK ABOUT 10 MINUTES
SERVES 4

1 Bring 1 inch water to a simmer in a medium skillet. Add the carrots and cook 5 minutes; add the sugar-snap peas and cook until the vegetables are crisp-tender, about 2 minutes. Drain in a colander.

2 Heat the oil in the skillet over medium-high heat. Add the cumin and curry powder; cook, stirring constantly, until fragrant, 15–20 seconds. Add the vegetables, lemon juice, honey, and salt; cook, stirring constantly, until heated through, 2–3 minutes.

PER SERVING (about ¾ cup): 56 Cal, 1 g Fat, 0 g Sat Fat, 0 g Trans Fat, 0 mg Chol, 168 mg Sod, 10 g Carb, 3 g Fib, 2 g Prot, 34 mg Calc. *POINTS* value: *1.*

GOOD IDEA This Moroccan-inspired vegetable dish pairs beautifully with couscous (⅔ cup cooked couscous for each serving will increase the *POINTS* value by 2).

1 (½-pound) package baby carrots, halved lengthwise

¼ pound fresh sugar-snap peas (about 1½ cups), trimmed

1 teaspoon olive oil

1 teaspoon ground cumin

½ teaspoon curry powder

2 teaspoons fresh lemon juice

1 teaspoon honey

¼ teaspoon salt

Sesame-Walnut Mustard Greens

PREP 10 MINUTES
COOK ABOUT 20 MINUTES
SERVES 4

1 Heat a large nonstick skillet or wok over high heat until a drop of water sizzles. Add the peanut oil, swirl to coat the pan, then add the garlic. Stir-fry until just fragrant, about 15 seconds. Add the mustard greens and stir-fry until heated through, 1–2 minutes.

2 Sprinkle with the walnuts, soy sauce, and sesame oil; toss to coat.

PER SERVING (¾ cup): 84 Cal, 7 g Fat, 1 g Sat Fat, 0 g Trans Fat, 0 mg Chol, 118 mg Sod, 4 g Carb, 3 g Fib, 4 g Prot, 86 mg Calc. **POINTS** value: *2.*

GOOD IDEA Peppery mustard greens are a perfect match for the rich flavors of sesame and walnut, or substitute other assertive greens, such as collards and turnip greens, or broccoli rabe.

1 teaspoon peanut oil

1 garlic clove, minced

3 cups steamed mustard greens

¼ cup walnuts, toasted and coarsely chopped

2 teaspoons reduced-sodium soy sauce

1 teaspoon Asian (dark) sesame oil

Dry-Cooked Green Beans

PREP	15 MINUTES
COOK	ABOUT 20 MINUTES
SERVES	4

1 Whisk together the soy sauce, wine, the dissolved cornstarch, the sugar, and ¼ cup water in a small bowl until smooth; set aside.

2 Heat a large nonstick skillet or wok over high heat until a drop of water sizzles. Add 1 tablespoon of the oil, swirl to coat the pan, then add the beans in 2-cup batches. Stir-fry until lightly browned and the edges are crisp, 1–2 minutes per batch. As it is done, transfer each batch to a plate and keep warm.

3 Add the remaining 1 teaspoon oil to the skillet, swirl to coat the pan, then add the scallions. Stir-fry until softened, 3–4 minutes. Stir in the beans and the soy sauce mixture; cook, stirring gently, until the sauce thickens and coats the beans, about 1 minute. Sprinkle with the sesame seeds.

PER SERVING (1½ cups): 109 Cal, 5 g Fat, 1 g Sat Fat, 0 g Trans Fat, 0 mg Chol, 161 mg Sod, 14 g Carb, 3 g Fib, 3 g Prot, 75 mg Calc. **POINTS** value: *2*.

FOOD NOTE For most Chinese cooks, peanut oil is the preferred oil for stir-frying. Unlike other oils, such as olive oil, it is able to heat to a high temperature without burning. If you do not have peanut oil, corn oil is a good substitute.

1 tablespoon reduced-sodium soy sauce

1 tablespoon rice wine or dry sherry

1 teaspoon cornstarch, dissolved in 1 tablespoon water

½ teaspoon sugar

1 tablespoon + 1 teaspoon peanut oil

6 cups fresh green beans, trimmed and steamed until crisp-tender

4 scallions, thinly sliced

1 teaspoon sesame seeds

Core Plan
Recipes

CHAPTER 8

Fennel-Crusted
Flank Steak

Fennel-Crusted Flank Steak

PREP	5 MINUTES PLUS 5 MINUTES STANDING TIME
COOK	ABOUT 10 MINUTES
SERVES	4

1 Combine the fennel, thyme, rosemary, garlic, salt, and pepper in a small bowl.

2 Heat a large nonstick skillet over high heat.

3 Meanwhile, rub the fennel mixture onto both sides of the steak. Add the steak to the skillet and cook until an instant-read thermometer inserted in the center registers 145°F for medium-rare, 4–5 minutes on each side. Transfer the steak to a cutting board and let stand about 5 minutes. Slice thinly on an angle across the grain into 12–16 slices.

PER SERVING (3–4 slices of steak): 168 Cal, 9 g Fat, 4 g Sat Fat, 0 g Trans Fat, 49 mg Chol, 632 mg Sod, 1 g Carb, 1 g Fib, 20 g Prot, 26 mg Calc. **POINTS** value: **4.**

1 tablespoon **fennel seeds**, crushed

1 teaspoon chopped **fresh thyme**

1 teaspoon chopped **fresh rosemary**

1 **garlic clove**, minced

1 teaspoon **salt**

½ teaspoon coarsely ground **black pepper**

1 (1-pound) **flank steak**, trimmed

HOW WE DID IT Be sure to let the steak rest for a few minutes before you slice it—slicing right out of the skillet causes the juices to run, leaving the meat dry.

Penne with Tomato and Olive-Meat Sauce

PREP 10 MINUTES
COOK ABOUT 25 MINUTES
SERVES 4

☑

1 To make the sauce, spray a large nonstick skillet with olive oil nonstick spray and set over medium-high heat. Add the beef, salt, cinnamon, and crushed red pepper; cook, breaking up the beef with a wooden spoon, until browned, about 5 minutes. Add the garlic and cook, stirring constantly, until fragrant, about 1 minute. Add the tomatoes and olives; bring to a boil, breaking up the tomatoes the spoon. Reduce the heat and simmer until the sauce is slightly thickened and the flavors are blended, about 15 minutes.

2 Meanwhile, cook the penne according to package directions omitting the salt, if desired; drain. Toss the penne with the sauce and parsley in a large serving bowl.

PER SERVING (1¾ cups): 387 Cal, 9 g Fat, 2 g Sat Fat, 0 g Trans Fat, 47 mg Chol, 924 mg Sod, 51 g Carb, 7 g Fib, 28 g Prot, 75 mg Calc. *POINTS* value: *8.*

EXPRESS LANE This sauce freezes beautifully. Make a double batch in a Dutch oven, then freeze half in an airtight container up to 2 months to use for another meal.

¾ **pound ground lean beef (7% or less fat)**

½ **teaspoon salt**

½ **teaspoon cinnamon**

¼ **teaspoon crushed red pepper**

2 **garlic cloves, crushed through a press**

1 **(28-ounce) can Italian tomatoes with basil**

15 **pitted kalamata olives, coarsely chopped**

½ **pound whole-wheat penne**

2 **tablespoons chopped fresh flat-leaf parsley**

Roast Chicken Salad

PREP 10 MINUTES
COOK ABOUT 5 MINUTES
SERVES 4

1 Heat the oil in a large nonstick skillet over medium-high heat. Add the bell pepper, carrot, garlic, and crushed red pepper; cook, stirring constantly, until the bell pepper is softened and the garlic is lightly golden, 1–2 minutes. Remove from the heat; stir in the chicken, lemon juice, and olives.

2 Divide the arugula among 4 salad plates; top with the chicken mixture.

PER SERVING (¾ cup salad with 2 arugula leaves): 165 Cal, 7 g Fat, 1 g Sat Fat, 0 g Trans Fat, 48 mg Chol, 115 mg Sod, 9 g Carb, 2 g Fib, 19 g Prot, 61 mg Calc. **POINTS** value: **3.**

FOOD NOTE Roast turkey breast from the deli case substitutes for chicken easily in this recipe, as does chopped celery in place of the carrot (the per-serving **POINTS** value will remain the same).

1 tablespoon olive oil

1 red bell pepper, seeded and diced

1 carrot, shredded

2 garlic cloves, minced

¼ teaspoon crushed red pepper

2 cups shredded roast skinless chicken breast

¼ cup fresh lemon juice

6 large green olives, pitted and sliced

8 arugula or radicchio leaves

Garlicky Seared Lamb Chops with Mint Vinaigrette

PREP	15 MINUTES
COOK	ABOUT 5 MINUTES
SERVES	4

1 To make the vinaigrette, combine the broth, oil, shallot, garlic, lemon zest, lemon juice, mint, oregano, and ¼ teaspoon of the salt in a bowl; set aside.

2 Sprinkle both sides of the lamb chops with the remaining ½ teaspoon salt and the pepper.

3 Spray a large nonstick skillet with nonstick spray and set over high heat. Add the lamb and cook until an instant-read thermometer inserted in the center of each chop registers 145°F for medium-rare, about 3 minutes on each side. Transfer the lamb to a platter. Stir and spoon the vinaigrette over the lamb.

PER SERVING (1 lamb chop with 2 tablespoons vinaigrette): 143 Cal, 8 g Fat, 2 g Sat Fat, 1 g Trans Fat, 45 mg Chol, 508 mg Sod, 2 g Carb, 1 g Fib, 15 g Prot, 32 mg Calc. **POINTS** value: **3.**

GOOD IDEA If you want to add a little richness to the dish, sprinkle each chop with 2 tablespoons crumbled feta cheese, increase the **POINTS** value per serving by 1½, and deduct it from your **weekly POINTS Allowance.**

3 tablespoons reduced-sodium chicken broth

1 tablespoon olive oil

1 shallot, minced

1 garlic clove, minced

1 tablespoon grated lemon zest

1 tablespoon fresh lemon juice

¼ cup chopped fresh mint

1 teaspoon dried oregano

¾ teaspoon salt

4 (¼-pound) bone-in loin lamb chops, trimmed

½ teaspoon coarsely ground black pepper

Garlicky Seared Lamb Chops with Mint Vinaigrette

Smoked Chicken and
New Potato Hash

Smoked Chicken and New Potato Hash

PREP	15 MINUTES
COOK	ABOUT 25 MINUTES
SERVES	4

☑

1 Heat 2 teaspoons of the oil in a large nonstick skillet over medium-high heat. Add the potatoes and cook, stirring frequently, about 2 minutes. Add the water, onion, bell peppers, paprika, fennel seeds, garlic powder, ½ teaspoon of the salt, and the ground pepper. Bring to a boil; cook, covered, shaking the pan occasionally, until the potatoes are just tender, about 15 minutes. Uncover and cook until the potatoes begin to brown slightly, about 5 minutes.

2 Meanwhile, toss the chicken, liquid smoke, and the remaining ¼ teaspoon salt in a medium bowl.

3 Heat the remaining 1 teaspoon oil in another large nonstick skillet over medium-high heat. Add the chicken and cook, stirring frequently, until cooked through, about 8 minutes. Stir the chicken into the hash.

PER SERVING (1 cup): 258 Cal, 5 g Fat, 1 g Sat Fat, 0 g Trans Fat, 49 mg Chol, 500 mg Sod, 31 g Carb, 4 g Fib, 23 g Prot, 37 mg Calc. **POINTS** value: **5.**

GOOD IDEA Looking to serve a hearty brunch? Add 1 poached egg to each serving of hash (you'll increase the per-serving **POINTS** value by 2).

3 teaspoons canola oil

1 pound red potatoes, scrubbed and sliced

1 cup water

1 onion, chopped

1 red bell pepper, seeded and chopped

1 green bell pepper, seeded and chopped

2 teaspoons paprika

½ teaspoon fennel seeds

½ teaspoon garlic powder

¾ teaspoon salt

¼ teaspoon coarsely ground black pepper

¾ pound skinless boneless chicken breasts, **cut into thin strips**

1 teaspoon liquid smoke

Pan-Seared Salmon with Fresh Tomato-Basil Relish

PREP	10 MINUTES
COOK	ABOUT 10 MINUTES
SERVES	2

1 To make the relish, combine the tomatoes, basil, vinegar, garlic, ½ teaspoon of the salt, and ⅛ teaspoon of the pepper in a small bowl; set aside.

2 Sprinkle both sides of the salmon with the cumin and the remaining ¼ teaspoon salt and ⅛ teaspoon pepper. Heat the oil in a large nonstick skillet over medium-high heat. Add the salmon, skin-side up, and cook about 4 minutes. Turn over the salmon and cook about 1 minute. Reduce the heat and cook, covered, until the salmon is just opaque in the center, 2–3 minutes.

3 Transfer the salmon to serving plates and add the relish to the skillet. Increase the heat and cook until the relish is heated through, 1–2 minutes. Spoon the relish over the salmon.

PER SERVING (1 salmon fillet with about ½ cup relish): 350 Cal, 19 g Fat, 4 g Sat Fat, 89 mg Chol, 0 g Trans Fat, 976 mg Sod, 10 g Carb, 2 g Fib, 33 g Prot, 44 mg Calc. **POINTS** value: **8.**

FOOD NOTE While this dish is best in the summer, when fresh tomatoes are at their peak, you can also use plum tomatoes or quartered cherry tomatoes other times of the year. Whatever the season, store tomatoes stem-side up at room temperature. Never refrigerate them, as cold destroys their texture and flavor.

Ingredients

- 2 ripe tomatoes, seeded and chopped
- ¼ cup thinly sliced fresh basil
- 1 tablespoon balsamic vinegar
- 1 small garlic clove, minced
- ¾ teaspoon salt
- ¼ teaspoon coarsely ground black pepper
- 2 (6-ounce) salmon fillets
- ¼ teaspoon ground cumin
- ½ teaspoon olive oil

Pan-Seared Salmon with
Fresh Tomato-Basil Relish

Poached Salmon with Dill-Mustard Sauce

PREP	15 MINUTES
COOK	ABOUT 20 MINUTES
SERVES	4

☑

1 Combine the clam juice, water, onion, carrot, celery, and bay leaf in a large skillet; bring to a boil. Reduce the heat and simmer, covered, until the flavors are blended, about 5 minutes. Add the salmon and simmer, uncovered, about 6 minutes. Turn the salmon over and simmer until just opaque in the center, about 3 minutes. Transfer the salmon to a plate and keep warm; discard the cooking liquid, vegetables, and bay leaf.

2 To make the sauce, meanwhile, combine the mayonnaise, dill, mustard, lemon juice, and pepper in a small bowl; set aside.

3 Wipe out the skillet with a paper towel and heat over medium-high heat. Add the spinach and cook with the water that clings to its leaves until just wilted, about 1 minute. Stir in the salt. Divide the spinach among 4 plates, place a salmon fillet on each, and drizzle with the sauce.

PER SERVING (1 salmon fillet with about ½ cup spinach and 2 tablespoons sauce): 236 Cal, 8 g Fat, 2 g Sat Fat, 0 g Trans Fat, 93 mg Chol, 550 mg Sod, 7 g Carb, 6 g Fib, 36 g Prot, 99 mg Calc. *POINTS* value: *5.*

EXPRESS LANE If you want to use convenient bagged baby spinach in this recipe, by all means do so, but rinse the greens in a colander before sautéeing, so that there is water clinging to the leaves and the spinach can wilt.

1 (8-ounce) bottle clam juice

1 cup water

1 onion, chopped

1 carrot, chopped

1 celery stalk, chopped

1 bay leaf

4 (6-ounce) skinless salmon fillets

½ cup fat-free mayonnaise

2 tablespoons chopped fresh dill

1 tablespoon Dijon mustard

1 tablespoon fresh lemon juice

⅛ teaspoon coarsely ground black pepper

8 cups baby spinach, cleaned (do not dry)

¼ teaspoon salt

Crispy Cornmeal Flounder

PREP	10 MINUTES
COOK	ABOUT 15 MINUTES
SERVES	4

1 Combine the cornmeal, parsley, oregano, Cajun seasoning, and salt on a large plate. Combine the egg whites and mustard in a large bowl; mix well.

2 Dip 1 fillet in the egg white mixture, then in the cornmeal mixture, pressing gently to coat. Place the fillet on a plate; repeat with the remaining fillets.

3 Heat 2 teaspoons of oil in a large nonstick skillet over medium-high heat. Add 2 fillets and cook until golden and the fillets are just opaque in the center, 3–4 minutes on each side. Transfer the fillets to a platter. Repeat with the remaining 2 teaspoons oil and 2 fillets. Serve with the salsa.

PER SERVING (1 flounder fillet with 2 tablespoons salsa): 283 Cal, 8 g Fat, 1 g Sat Fat, 0 g Trans Fat, 80 mg Chol, 987 mg Sod, 19 g Carb, 3 g Fib, 34 g Prot, 62 mg Calc. **POINTS** value: **6.**

½ cup cornmeal

¼ cup chopped fresh parsley

1 tablespoon chopped fresh oregano

2 teaspoons Cajun seasoning

½ teaspoon salt

2 egg whites, beaten

3 tablespoons Dijon mustard

4 (6-ounce) skinless flounder fillets

4 teaspoons olive oil

½ cup fat-free salsa

GOOD IDEA For a little touch of richness, stir half a medium avocado, peeled and diced, into the salsa before spooning it over the fish (you'll increase the per-serving **POINTS** value by 1).

Sea Bass with Dill Couscous

Sea Bass with Dill Couscous

PREP	15 MINUTES PLUS 5 MINUTES STANDING TIME
COOK	ABOUT 15 MINUTES
SERVES	6

1 Combine the cumin, coriander, cinnamon, ¼ teaspoon of the salt, and ⅛ teaspoon of the ground pepper in a bowl. Sprinkle the mixture on both sides of the fillets. Heat the oil in a large nonstick skillet over medium-high heat. Add the fillets, skin-side up, and cook until just opaque in the center, 3–4 minutes on each side. Transfer to a plate and keep warm.

2 Add the onion and tomatoes to the skillet; cook, stirring occasionally, until softened, about 3 minutes. Add the capers, 1 tablespoon of the lemon juice, ¼ teaspoon of the salt, and ⅛ teaspoon of the ground pepper; cook until the flavors are blended, about 1 minute. Remove from the heat.

3 Meanwhile, bring the water to a boil in a small saucepan. Remove the pan from the heat; stir in the couscous, bell pepper, and the remaining ½ teaspoon salt and ¼ teaspoon ground pepper. Cover and let stand until the water has been absorbed, about 5 minutes; stir in the mint, dill, and the remaining 2 tablespoons lemon juice. Spoon the tomato mixture over the fillets and serve with the couscous.

PER SERVING (1 sea bass fillet with about 1 tablespoon tomato mixture and ⅓ cup couscous): 329 Cal, 5 g Fat, 1 g Sat Fat, 0 g Trans Fat, 47 mg Chol, 520 mg Sod, 43 g Carb, 5 g Fib, 28 g Prot, 45 mg Calc. **POINTS** value: **6**.

FOOD NOTE You can substitute any mild, firm-fleshed white fish such as grouper or red snapper fillets, for the sea bass.

- 1 teaspoon ground cumin
- ½ teaspoon ground coriander
- ½ teaspoon cinnamon
- 1 teaspoon salt
- ½ teaspoon coarsely ground black pepper
- 6 (¼-pound) Chilean sea bass fillets
- 2 teaspoons olive oil
- 1 onion, chopped
- 1 pint cherry tomatoes, halved
- 1 tablespoon capers, drained
- 3 tablespoons fresh lemon juice
- 1¾ cups water
- 1½ cups couscous
- 1 red bell pepper, seeded and chopped
- 3 tablespoons chopped fresh mint
- 2 tablespoons chopped fresh dill

Shrimp and Scallop Paella

PREP 15 MINUTES
COOK ABOUT 45 MINUTES
SERVES 6 ✓

1 Heat the oil in a large nonstick skillet over medium-high heat. Add the shrimp and scallops; cook until browned, 1–1½ minutes on each side. Transfer to a plate and set aside.

2 Add the onion, bell pepper, and garlic to the skillet; cook, stirring occasionally, until the vegetables begin to soften, about 3 minutes. Stir in the saffron and cook, stirring frequently, until fragrant, about 30 seconds. Add the rice and cook, stirring frequently, until well-coated, about 1 minute. Stir in the broth, peas, salt, and ground pepper; bring to a boil. Reduce the heat and simmer, covered, until the liquid is almost absorbed and the rice is tender, about 30 minutes.

3 Increase the heat to high. Stir in the shrimp, scallops, and artichoke hearts; cook, stirring occasionally, until heated through, 3–4 minutes. Serve at once.

PER SERVING (about ¾ cup): 313 Cal, 7 g Fat, 1 g Sat Fat, 0 g Trans Fat, 112 mg Chol, 971 mg Sod, 36 g Carb, 5 g Fib, 27 g Prot, 51 mg Calc. **POINTS** value: **6.**

HOW WE DID IT Searing the shrimp and scallops is an important step in this recipe, because you want to lock in all the juices. So be sure to use a large nonstick skillet and not to overcrowd the pan so the seafood will brown (versus steam). If necessary, cook the shrimp and scallops in separate batches for best results.

1 tablespoon extra-virgin olive oil

¾ pound peeled and deveined large shrimp

¾ pound sea scallops

1 onion, chopped

1 red bell pepper, seeded and chopped

3 garlic cloves, minced

¼ teaspoon saffron, lightly crushed

1 cup brown rice

2½ cups reduced-sodium chicken broth

½ cup frozen peas

¾ teaspoon salt

¼ teaspoon freshly ground pepper

1 (14-ounce) can quartered artichoke hearts, drained

Seafood Linguine

PREP	15 MINUTES
COOK	ABOUT 20 MINUTES
SERVES	4

1 Heat the oil in a large nonstick skillet over medium-high heat. Add the garlic and crushed red pepper; cook, stirring constantly, until fragrant, about 30 seconds. Stir in the squid, scallops, and basil; cook, stirring constantly, about 1 minute. Add the spinach, tomatoes, lemon juice, lemon zest, salt, and ground pepper; cook, stirring constantly, until the spinach wilts and the seafood is just opaque in the center, about 2 minutes.

2 Meanwhile, cook the linguine according to package directions omitting the salt, if desired; drain. Toss the linguine and seafood mixture in a large serving bowl.

PER SERVING (1 ½ cups): 335 Cal, 4 g Fat, 1 g Sat Fat, 0 g Trans Fat, 127 mg Chol, 623 mg Sod, 49 g Carb, 9 g Fib, 27 g Prot, 68 mg Calc. **POINTS** value: *6.*

FOOD NOTE You can substitute an equal amount of shelled and deveined shrimp for the scallops or squid, if desired. (The cooking times will remain the same.)

2 teaspoons extra-virgin olive oil

1 large garlic clove, minced

Pinch crushed red pepper

½ pound cleaned squid, bodies sliced into rings

½ pound sea scallops, halved crosswise

¼ cup thinly sliced fresh basil

3 cups baby spinach, coarsely chopped

2 plum tomatoes, diced

Juice and grated zest of ½ lemon

¾ teaspoon salt

¼ teaspoon freshly ground pepper

½ (1-pound) box whole-wheat linguine

Polenta with Vegetarian Sausage-Tomato Sauce

PREP	10 MINUTES
COOK	ABOUT 15 MINUTES
SERVES	4

1 Heat the oil in a large nonstick skillet over medium-high heat. Add the onion, garlic, and fennel seeds; cook, stirring occasionally, until the onion begins to soften, 2–3 minutes. Stir in the soy burgers and cook, stirring occasionally, until browned, about 3 minutes. Add the tomatoes and tomato paste, reduce the heat and simmer, covered, until the sauce begins to thicken, about 10 minutes.

2 Meanwhile, combine the milk, water, salt, and pepper in a medium saucepan; bring to a boil over medium-high heat. Slowly pour in the polenta in a thin, steady stream whisking constantly. Cook, whisking constantly, until thick and creamy, 5–6 minutes. Remove the saucepan from the heat; stir in the cheese. Divide the polenta among 4 plates; top each serving with the tomato sauce.

PER SERVING (1 cup polenta and ½ cup sauce): 379 Cal, 5 g Fat, 1 g Sat Fat, 0 g Trans Fat, 14 mg Chol, 1,136 mg Sod, 57 g Carb, 8 g Fib, 27 g Prot, 372 mg Calc. *POINTS* value: *7.*

HOW WE DID IT Allow the frozen soy burgers to stand at room temperature 10 minutes to soften slightly, and they'll be easier to chop.

2 teaspoons olive oil

1 onion, chopped

3 garlic cloves, minced

½ teaspoon fennel seeds

2 frozen grilled vegetable soy burgers, chopped

1 (14-ounce) can whole tomatoes, chopped

3 tablespoons tomato paste

3 cups fat-free milk

1 cup water

1 teaspoon salt

¼ teaspoon freshly ground pepper

¾ cup instant polenta

1 cup fat-free ricotta cheese

Scrambled Tofu with Vegetables

PREP 15 MINUTES
COOK ABOUT 15 MINUTES
SERVES 4

1 Heat the oil in a large nonstick skillet over medium-high heat. Add the mushrooms, scallions, bell pepper, and garlic; cook, stirring occasionally, until the vegetables are softened, 10–12 minutes.

2 Stir in the tofu, salt, and ground pepper; cook, stirring occasionally, until the tofu is heated through and the flavors are blended, about 5 minutes. Stir in the basil and parsley.

PER SERVING (about 1 cup): 128 Cal, 8 g Fat, 1 g Sat Fat, 0 g Trans Fat, 0 mg Chol, 304 mg Sod, 8 g Carb, 2 g Fib, 7 g Prot, 47 mg Calc. *POINTS* value: *3.*

GOOD IDEA Serve this simple tofu dish for brunch or dinner with a crisp green salad tossed with your favorite fat-free dressing.

4 teaspoons **olive oil**

2 cups chopped **fresh mushrooms**

8 **scallions,** sliced

1 **red bell pepper,** seeded and diced

1 **garlic clove,** minced

1 pound **reduced-fat soft tofu,** diced

½ teaspoon **salt**

¼ teaspoon freshly **ground pepper**

2 tablespoons chopped **fresh basil**

2 tablespoons chopped **fresh flat-leaf parsley**

Pipérade

PREP 20 MINUTES
COOK ABOUT 25 MINUTES
SERVES 4

☑ 🥕

1 Heat 2 teaspoons of the oil in a medium nonstick skillet over medium-high heat. Add the tomatoes, reduce the heat, and simmer, stirring occasionally, until softened, about 10 minutes (watch for burning).

2 Meanwhile, heat the remaining 2 teaspoons oil in a large nonstick skillet over medium heat. Add the bell peppers, onions, chile, and garlic; cook, stirring occasionally, until softened, about 15 minutes. Stir in the tomatoes, oregano, marjoram, salt, and pepper; cook, stirring occasionally, until the flavors are blended, about 5 minutes. Pour in the eggs; cook, stirring frequently, until the eggs are set, 2–3 minutes.

PER SERVING (about 1 cup): 202 Cal, 10 g Fat, 2 g Sat Fat, 0 g Trans Fat, 212 mg Chol, 83 mg Sod, 20 g Carb, 4 g Fib, 9 g Prot, 65 mg Calc. **POINTS** value: **4.**

GOOD IDEA *Pipérade* (pee-pay-RAHD), a French egg specialty from the Basque region, is a divine way to savor the bounty of sweet bell peppers and juicy tomatoes in the summer. Or, omit the eggs to make a delightful side dish (and reduce the per-serving **POINTS** value by 2).

4 teaspoons olive oil

6 tomatoes, cut into 1-inch chunks

3 green bell peppers, seeded and cut into 1-inch pieces

2 onions, chopped

1 mild green chile (Anaheim or poblano), seeded and sliced

2 garlic cloves, minced

1 teaspoon dried oregano

½ teaspoon dried marjoram

Pinch salt

Freshly ground pepper to taste

4 large eggs, beaten

Mushroom and Cheese Omelette

PREP	10 MINUTES
COOK	ABOUT 10 MINUTES
SERVES	4

1 Spray a medium nonstick skillet with nonstick spray and set over high heat. Add the leek and cook, stirring constantly, until it just starts to brown, about 2 minutes. Add the mushrooms and cook, stirring frequently, until well browned, about 3 minutes. Transfer the vegetables to a bowl and stir in the cheese.

2 To make the sauce, puree the roasted peppers, tomato paste, ground pepper, and thyme in a food processor or blender.

3 Spray a large nonstick skillet with nonstick cooking spray and set over medium-high heat until smoking. Pour in the egg substitute and swirl to cover the pan. Cook, stirring gently, until the underside is set, 2–3 minutes. Spread the vegetables evenly over half of the omelette; fold the other half over the filling. Slide the omelette onto a plate and pour the sauce on top. Cut into 4 wedges.

PER SERVING (1 wedge with about ¼ cup sauce): 70 Cal, 0 g Fat, 0 g Sat Fat, 0 g Trans Fat, 0 mg Chol, 260 mg Sod, 10 g Carb, 1 g Fib, 8 g Prot, 49 mg Calc. **POINTS** value: *1.*

1 leek, trimmed to white and light-green parts, cleaned, and sliced

1¼ cups chopped fresh shiitake mushrooms

2 tablespoons crumbled fat-free feta cheese

1 (7-ounce) jar roasted red peppers, rinsed and drained

1 tablespoon tomato paste

¼ teaspoon coarsely ground black pepper

¼ teaspoon dried thyme

1 cup fat-free egg substitute, beaten until frothy

Indian Lentil and Vegetable Stew

PREP 10 MINUTES
COOK ABOUT 40 MINUTES
SERVES 4

1 Combine 1 cup of the water, the lentils, and turmeric in a medium saucepan; bring to a boil. Reduce the heat and simmer, covered, until the lentils are soft, about 30 minutes. Transfer to a blender or food processor and puree.

2 Meanwhile, heat the oil in a large nonstick skillet over medium-high heat. Add the mustard seeds and cook, covered, until the popping subsides, 1–2 minutes. Add the garlic and chile; cook, stirring frequently, until fragrant, about 1 minute. Stir in the Brussels sprouts, tomatoes, the remaining ³/₄ cup water, and the salt; cook, covered, until the Brussels sprouts are tender, about 10 minutes.

3 Stir the pureed lentils into the vegetables; cook until heated through, about 5 minutes. Remove the skillet from the heat; stir in the lemon juice and cilantro.

PER SERVING (about 1 cup): 205 Cal, 6 g Fat, 1 g Sat Fat, 0 g Trans Fat, 0 mg Chol, 350 mg Sod, 31 g Carb, 6 g Fiber, 10 g Prot, 107 mg Calc. **POINTS** value: **4.**

FOOD NOTE If you're sensitive to hot and spicy foods, by all means seed and devein the chile— although including the seeds gives this dish a more authentic flavor.

1³/₄ cups water

½ cup yellow lentils or yellow split peas, picked over, rinsed, and drained

½ teaspoon turmeric

4 teaspoons canola oil

2 teaspoons mustard seeds

3 garlic cloves, minced

1 serrano chile, thinly sliced (wear gloves to prevent irritation)

1 (10-ounce) package frozen Brussels sprouts, thawed

1 cup canned diced tomatoes (no salt added)

½ teaspoon salt

1 tablespoon fresh lemon juice

1 tablespoon chopped fresh cilantro

Indian Lentil and
Vegetable Stew

Tuscan-Style Escarole and Cannellini Beans

PREP 10 MINUTES
COOK ABOUT 25 MINUTES
SERVES 6

1 Combine the escarole, broth, onion, and garlic in a Dutch oven; bring to a boil over medium-high heat. Cook, stirring frequently, until the escarole wilts, about 3 minutes. Reduce the heat and simmer, covered, until the escarole is almost tender, about 3 minutes.

2 Stir in the beans, tomatoes, fennel seeds, and crushed red pepper; bring to a boil. Reduce the heat and simmer, uncovered, until the escarole is tender and most of the liquid evaporates, about 10 minutes. Remove the Dutch oven from the heat; stir in the oil.

PER SERVING (¾ cup): 104 Cal, 2 g Fat, 0 g Sat Fat, 0 g Trans Fat, 0 mg Chol, 348 mg Sod, 17 g Carb, 6 g Fib, 5 g Prot, 76 mg Calc. **POINTS** value: *1.*

EXPRESS LANE If you happen to have any leftovers, add a little chicken broth to make a delicious escarole and bean soup for a quick lunch (1 cup broth for each serving will keep the **POINTS** value the same).

1 medium head escarole (about 1 pound), trimmed and torn into bite-size pieces

1 cup reduced-sodium chicken broth

1 onion, chopped

4 garlic cloves, sliced

1 (19-ounce) can cannellini (white kidney) beans, rinsed and drained

1 (14½-ounce) can diced fire-roasted tomatoes

1 teaspoon fennel seeds

⅛ teaspoon crushed red pepper

2 teaspoons extra-virgin olive oil

Spiced Barley Pilaf

PREP 15 MINUTES
COOK ABOUT 55 MINUTES
SERVES 6

✓

1 Heat a large skillet over medium heat. Add the barley and toast, stirring occasionallly, until fragrant, about 5 minutes. Transfer to a plate and set aside.

2 Heat the oil in a large saucepan over medium-high heat. Add the carrots, red onion, and celery; cook, covered, stirring occasionally, until softened, about 5 minutes. Stir in the garlic, bay leaf, cumin, salt, paprika, turmeric, and pepper; cook, stirring frequently, until fragrant, about 30 seconds. Add the barley, broth, and water; bring to a boil. Reduce the heat and simmer, covered, until the barley is tender and the liquid is absorbed, about 40 minutes. Discard the bay leaf before serving.

PER SERVING (⅔ cup): 151 Cal, 2 g Fat, 0 g Sat Fat, 0 g Trans Fat, 0 mg Chol, 502 mg Sod, 30 g Carb, 6 g Fib, 5 g Prot, 24 mg Calc. **POINTS** value: *2.*

GOOD IDEA Sprinkle each serving with 1 tablespoon grated Parmesan cheese, increase the **POINTS** value by ½, and deduct it from your **weekly POINTS** Allowance.

1 **cup** pearl barley

2 **teaspoons** canola oil

2 **small** carrots, **diced**

1 **small** red onion, **diced**

1 celery stalk, **diced**

2 garlic cloves, **minced**

½ **bay leaf**

1 **teaspoon**
   ground cumin

¾ **teaspoon** salt

½ **teaspoon** paprika

¼ **teaspoon** turmeric

¼ **teaspoon freshly**
   ground pepper

1 (14½-ounce) can
   reduced-sodium
   chicken broth

¾ **cup** water

Chickpea, Asparagus, and Corn Sauté

PREP 15 MINUTES
COOK ABOUT 10 MINUTES
SERVES 4

1 Heat the oil in a large nonstick skillet over medium-high heat. Add the garlic and cook, stirring constantly, until fragrant, about 30 seconds. Add the corn and cook, stirring occasionally, until it begins to brown, 2–3 minutes. Add the asparagus and cook, stirring occasionally, until bright green, 3–4 minutes. Add the chickpeas and cook, stirring occasionally, until the asparagus is tender, 2–3 minutes.

2 Remove the skillet from the heat; stir in the tomatoes, red onion, basil, salt, and pepper.

PER SERVING (1 cup): 171 Cal, 5 g Fat, 1 g Sat Fat, 0 g Trans Fat, 0 mg Chol, 435 mg Sod, 27 g Carb, 6 g Fib, 7 g Prot, 48 mg Calc. *POINTS* value: *3.*

GOOD IDEA Serve this easy sauté at once or at room temperature with brown rice (½ cup cooked rice for each serving will increase the *POINTS* value by 2).

1 tablespoon extra-virgin olive oil

3 garlic cloves, minced

1½ cups fresh or thawed frozen corn kernels

1 pound fresh asparagus, trimmed and cut into 1½-inch pieces

1 (15½-ounce) can chickpeas, rinsed and drained

1 cup cherry tomatoes, halved

½ small red onion, finely chopped

¼ cup thinly sliced fresh basil

½ teaspoon salt

¼ teaspoon freshly ground pepper

Edamame and Shiitake Mushroom Sauté

PREP 10 MINUTES
COOK ABOUT 10 MINUTES
SERVES 4

1 Heat the oil in a large nonstick skillet over medium-high heat. Add the onion, garlic, and ginger; cook, stirring frequently, until softened, about 2 minutes. Add the water and cook, stirring to scrape the brown bits from the skillet. Add the edamame; reduce the heat and simmer, covered, 2 minutes. Add the mushrooms and cook, uncovered, stirring frequently, until the mushrooms and edamame are tender, about 6 minutes.

2 Remove the skillet from the heat; stir in the soy sauce and serve at once.

PER SERVING (¾ cup): 117 Cal, 4 g Fat, 0 g Sat Fat, 0 g Trans Fat, 0 mg Chol, 175 mg Sod, 12 g Carb, 4 g Fib, 8 g Prot, 44 mg Calc. **POINTS** value: *2.*

- 1½ teaspoons canola oil
- ½ cup chopped onion
- 2 garlic cloves, minced
- 1 teaspoon grated peeled fresh ginger
- ¾ cup water
- 1½ cups frozen shelled edamame (green soybeans)
- ½ pound fresh shiitake mushrooms, stems discarded and sliced
- 1 tablespoon reduced-sodium soy sauce

TRY IT *Edamame* (eh-dah-MAH-meh)—the Japanese word for green soybeans—are now available shelled and frozen in most natural-foods stores and some supermarkets. Their slightly nutty flavor and chewy texture are perfect in this nutritious skillet dish.

Cannellini Bean and
Escarole Stew

Cannellini Bean and Escarole Stew

PREP 10 MINUTES
COOK ABOUT 20 MINUTES
SERVES 4

Heat the oil in a large nonstick skillet over medium-high heat. Add the onions and cook, stirring frequently, until softened, about 5 minutes. Add the escarole, garlic, salt, and pepper; cook, stirring occasionally, until the escarole is wilted, about 3 minutes. Stir in the beans and tomatoes; simmer, covered, until the flavors are blended, about 10 minutes.

PER SERVING (about ¾ cup): 142 Cal, 3 g Fat, 0 g Sat Fat, 0 g Trans Fat, 0 mg Chol, 490 mg Sod, 24 g Carb, 7 g Fib, 7 g Prot, 104 mg Calc. *POINTS* value: *2.*

TRY IT Escarole (broad-leaf endive), a green related to chicory but not nearly as bitter, is flavorful in salads, lightly sautéed, or eaten raw. The escarole will wilt quite a bit when cooked in this recipe, so don't worry about chopping it too fine—2-inch pieces are about right.

2 **teaspoons** olive oil

2 onions, **chopped**

1 **bunch** escarole, **cleaned and chopped**

3 garlic cloves, **minced**

½ **teaspoon** salt

½ **teaspoon freshly** ground pepper

1 **(15-ounce) can** cannellini (white kidney) beans, **rinsed and drained**

1 **(14-ounce) can** diced tomatoes **(no salt added)**

Warm White Bean Salad

PREP	10 MINUTES
COOK	ABOUT 5 MINUTES
SERVES	4

Heat the oil in a medium nonstick skillet. Add the tomatoes, onion, sage, garlic, salt, and pepper; cook, stirring occasionally, until the sauce thickens, about 5 minutes. Stir in the beans.

PER SERVING (about 1 cup): 138 Cal, 5 g Fat, 1 g Sat Fat, 0 g Trans Fat, 0 mg Chol, 264 mg Sod, 18 g Carb, 6 g Fib, 6 g Prot, 40 mg Calc. *POINTS* value: *2.*

GOOD IDEA This salad makes an ideal stuffing for peppers: Halve and seed 4 red bell peppers, stuff each with 1 cup of the bean salad, then bake at 425°F until tender, about 30 minutes. The per-serving *POINTS* value will remain the same.

4 teaspoons olive oil

4 plum tomatoes, chopped

1 onion, minced

2 tablespoons minced fresh sage, or 1 teaspoon dried

1 garlic clove, minced

¼ teaspoon salt

¼ teaspoon freshly ground pepper

1 (16-ounce) can cannellini (white kidney) beans, rinsed and drained

Curried Cauliflower with Black Beans

PREP	10 MINUTES
COOK	ABOUT 20 MINUTES
SERVES	4

1 Heat the oil in a large nonstick skillet over medium-high heat. Add the curry powder, cumin, and coriander; cook, stirring constantly, until just fragrant, 10–15 seconds. Add the cauliflower, 1/4 cup of the water, and the crushed red pepper; cook, stirring occasionally, until the cauliflower is well-coated and nearly all the liquid evaporates, 3–4 minutes.

2 Add the tomatoes and the remaining 1/4 cup water; cook, covered, stirring occasionally, until slightly thickened, about 10 minutes. Gently stir in the beans; cook until heated through, 2–3 minutes. Sprinkle with the cilantro.

PER SERVING (about 1 1/4 cups): 176 Cal, 6 g Fat, 1 g Sat Fat, 0 g Trans Fat, 0 mg Chol, 274 mg Sod, 26 g Carb, 10 g Fib, 9 g Prot, 82 mg Calc. **POINTS** value: **3.**

EXPRESS LANE To save on prep time, use a 1-pound bag of precut cauliflower florets. You'll find it in the produce aisle of the supermarket. This curry tastes even better the next day so double the recipe for another meal.

- 4 teaspoons canola oil
- 1 teaspoon curry powder
- 1/2 teaspoon ground cumin
- 1/2 teaspoon ground coriander
- 1 small cauliflower, cored and separated into florets
- 1/2 cup water
- 1/2 teaspoon crushed red pepper
- 1 (14-ounce) can crushed tomatoes (no salt added)
- 1 (19-ounce) can black beans, rinsed and drained
- 2 tablespoons minced fresh cilantro

Minted Succotash

PREP 15 MINUTES
COOK ABOUT 15 MINUTES
SERVES 4

Heat the oil in a large skillet over medium-high heat. Add the bell pepper, onion, and garlic; cook, stirring frequently, until softened, about 5 minutes. Add the corn, beans, and water; simmer, covered, until tender, about 10 minutes. Stir in the mint, salt, and ground pepper. Serve at once.

PER SERVING (about ¾ cup): 122 Cal, 3 g Fat, 0 g Sat Fat, 0 g Trans Fat, 0 mg Chol, 174 mg Sod, 22 g Carb, 6 g Fib, 5 g Prot, 23 mg Calc. **POINTS** value: **2.**

FOOD NOTE You'll need 2 medium corn-on-the-cobs to yield 1 cup kernels and ¾ pound unshelled lima beans to yield 1 cup shelled beans for this recipe. Serve this classic vegetable dish with roast chicken, if desired.

2 teaspoons canola oil

1 red bell pepper, seeded and diced

1 onion, diced

½ garlic clove, minced

1 cup fresh or thawed frozen corn kernels

1 cup fresh or thawed frozen lima beans

1 cup water

1 tablespoon chopped fresh mint

¼ teaspoon salt

¼ teaspoon freshly ground pepper

Minted Succotash

Fragrant Rice and Black-Eyed Pea Sauté

PREP	15 MINUTES
COOK	ABOUT 10 MINUTES
SERVES	4

1 Heat the oil in a large nonstick skillet over medium-high heat. Add the onion and cook, stirring frequently, until softened, about 5 minutes. Add the tomatoes and cook, stirring frequently, until softened, about 1 minute.

2 Stir in the rice, peas, parsley, basil, rosemary, and thyme; cook, tossing gently, until heated through, about 3 minutes. Stir in the lemon juice, salt, and pepper.

PER SERVING (about 1 cup): 235 Cal, 4 g Fat, 1 g Sat Fat, 0 g Trans Fat, 0 mg Chol, 515 mg Sod, 43 g Carb, 5 g Fib, 8 g Prot, 65 mg Calc. *POINTS* value: *4.*

FOOD NOTE If you prefer to use fresh, dried, or frozen black-eyed peas, substitute 1½ cups cooked peas for the canned.

2 teaspoons olive oil

1 onion, chopped

4 plum tomatoes, diced

2 cups cooked brown rice

1 (15-ounce) can black-eyed peas, rinsed and drained

3 tablespoons chopped fresh flat-leaf parsley

1 tablespoon chopped fresh basil

2 teaspoons minced fresh rosemary

1 teaspoon minced fresh thyme

2 tablespoons fresh lemon juice

½ teaspoon salt

¼ teaspoon freshly ground pepper

Vegetable Fried Rice

PREP	15 MINUTES
COOK	ABOUT 15 MINUTES
SERVES	4

1 Place the rice in a shallow bowl. With moistened fingers, stir the rice to separate the grains.

2 Heat the oil in a large nonstick skillet over medium-high heat. Add the bell pepper and scallions; cook, stirring frequently, until the vegetables begin to soften, 2–3 minutes. Stir in the rice and ginger; cook, stirring frequently, until heated through, 5–6 minutes.

3 Push the rice mixture to the sides of the skillet; add the eggs to the center and cook, stirring constantly, until softly scrambled, about 1 minute. Continue to stir, incorporating the rice. Stir in the cabbage, beans, and soy sauce; cook, stirring constantly, until the cabbage is wilted, 2–3 minutes.

PER SERVING (about 1 cup): 268 Cal, 8 g Fat, 1 g Sat Fat, 0 g Trans Fat, 106 mg Chol, 192 mg Sod, 42 g Carb, 4 g Fib, 8 g Prot, 64 mg Calc. **POINTS** value: **5.**

GOOD IDEA For extra crunch, sprinkle each serving with 1½ teaspoons toasted sesame seeds, increase the **POINTS** value by ½, and deduct it from your **weekly POINTS Allowance**.

3 cups cold cooked brown rice

4 teaspoons canola oil

1 red bell pepper, seeded and diced

8 scallions, thinly sliced

2 teaspoons grated peeled fresh ginger

2 large eggs, lightly beaten

1 cup shredded napa cabbage

¼ pound fresh green beans, trimmed, steamed, and cut into 1-inch pieces

1 tablespoon reduced-sodium soy sauce

Potato and Broccoli Rabe Skillet Pie

PREP 15 MINUTES
COOK ABOUT 55 MINUTES
SERVES 4

1 Heat 2 teaspoons of the oil in a large nonstick skillet over medium-high heat. Add the onion and cook, stirring frequently, until softened, about 5 minutes. Add the broccoli rabe, garlic, and fennel seeds; cook, stirring occasionally, until the broccoli rabe is wilted, about 5 minutes. Transfer to a plate.

2 Remove the skillet from the heat; add the remaining 2 teaspoons oil. Arrange half the potato slices in the bottom of the skillet, overlapping if necessary. Sprinkle with ¼ teaspoon of the salt and ⅛ teaspoon of the pepper. Spoon the broccoli rabe over the potatoes. Cover with the remaining potatoes; sprinkle with the remaining ¼ teaspoon salt and ⅛ teaspoon pepper. Cover the potatoes with a heat-proof plate to weight them down. Reduce the heat and cook, covered, until the potatoes are cooked through and the bottoms are browned, 40–45 minutes. Invert the pie onto a serving platter and cut into 4 wedges.

PER SERVING (1 wedge): 175 Cal, 5 g Fat, 1 g Sat Fat, 0 g Trans Fat, 0 mg Chol, 336 mg Sod, 29 g Carb, 6 g Fib, 7 g Prot, 83 mg Calc. **POINTS** value: **3.**

4 teaspoons olive oil

1 onion, sliced

1 bunch broccoli rabe, trimmed and coarsely chopped

2 garlic cloves, minced

½ teaspoon fennel seeds

4 small all-purpose potatoes, peeled and thinly sliced

½ teaspoon salt

¼ teaspoon freshly ground pepper

TRY IT Leafy green broccoli rabe is related to both the cabbage and turnip families. It typically has 6- to 9-inch stalks and scattered clusters of tiny broccoli-like buds. Broccoli rabe can be found from fall to spring in many supermarkets. It should be wrapped in a plastic bag and refrigerated up to 5 days.

Summer Harvest Stew

PREP	10 MINUTES
COOK	ABOUT 10 MINUTES
SERVES	4

1 Heat the oil in a large nonstick skillet over medium-high heat. Add the onions and cook, stirring occasionally, until softened, about 5 minutes. Add the garlic and cook, stirring constantly, until fragrant, about 1 minute.

2 Stir in the tomatoes, okra, corn, broth, salt, and pepper; bring to a boil. Reduce the heat and simmer, stirring occasionally, until the okra is tender, about 5 minutes. Stir in the basil.

PER SERVING (about 1¼ cups): 164 Cal, 5 g Fat, 1 g Sat Fat, 0 g Trans Fat, 0 mg Chol, 221 mg Sod, 27 g Carb, 5 g Fib, 5 g Prot, 54 mg Calc. *POINTS* value: *3.*

GOOD IDEA When buying fresh okra, look for firm, brightly colored pods less than 4 inches long. Larger pods may be tough and fibrous.

4 teaspoons extra-virgin olive oil

2 onions, coarsely chopped

2 garlic cloves, minced

2 tomatoes, coarsely chopped

2 cups fresh or thawed frozen okra, cut into ½-inch pieces

2 cups fresh or thawed frozen corn kernels

1 cup vegetable broth

¼ teaspoon salt

¼ teaspoon freshly ground pepper

2 tablespoons chopped fresh basil

Caribbean Gingery Squash, Rice, and Kale

PREP   20 MINUTES PLUS 5 MINUTES STANDING TIME
COOK   ABOUT 45 MINUTES
SERVES   4   ✓ 🥕

1 Heat the oil in a large nonstick skillet over medium-high heat. Add the onion and cook, stirring frequently, until softened, about 5 minutes. Add the squash, jalapeños, ginger, garlic, curry powder, cloves, and allspice; cook, stirring frequently, until the vegetables are well coated with the spices, about 1 minute.

2 Add the kale in handfuls, stirring as it wilts. Stir in the water, rice, salt, and ground pepper; bring to a boil. Reduce the heat and simmer, covered, until the rice is tender and the water is absorbed, 35–40 minutes. Remove from the heat; add the lime juice and fluff with a fork. Let stand, covered, 5 minutes.

PER SERVING (about 1¼ cups): 251 Cal, 6 g Fat, 1 g Sat Fat, 0 g Trans Fat, 0 mg Chol, 647 mg Sod, 45 g Carb, 6 g Fib, 6 g Prot, 146 mg Calc. **POINTS** value: **5.**

FOOD NOTE Look for butternut squash that are heavy for their size and have a good hard skin. Tender skin indicates that a squash has been picked before it was totally ripe and therefore has yet to develop its full flavor. Check to see that there are no discolorations or soft spots. Generally, the smaller the squash the better the flavor—and the easier to prepare and cook.

- 4 teaspoons canola oil
- 1 onion, chopped
- 1 (2-pound) butternut squash, peeled, seeded, and cut into 2-inch chunks
- 2 jalapeño peppers, seeded and minced (wear gloves to prevent irritation)
- 2 teaspoons grated peeled fresh ginger
- 3 garlic cloves, minced
- 1 teaspoon curry powder
- Pinch ground cloves
- Pinch ground allspice
- 1 bunch kale, cleaned and chopped
- 1½ cups water
- ⅔ cup brown rice
- 1 teaspoon salt
- ¼ teaspoon freshly ground pepper
- 2 tablespoons fresh lime juice

Caribbean Gingery Squash,
Rice, and Kale

Sautéed Zucchini with Lemon, Olives, and Oregano

PREP   10 MINUTES
COOK   ABOUT 10 MINUTES
SERVES 4

1 Heat the oil in a large nonstick skillet over medium-high heat. Add the zucchini and onion; cook, stirring frequently, until the vegetables are tender and light golden, about 8 minutes.

2 Add the garlic, salt, and crushed red pepper; cook, stirring constantly, until fragrant, about 1 minute. Remove the skillet from the heat; stir in the olives, lemon juice, oregano, and lemon zest.

PER SERVING (¾ cup): 43 Cal, 2 g Fat, 0 g Sat Fat, 0 g Trans Fat, 0 mg Chol, 210 mg Sod, 5 g Carb, 2 g Fib, 2 g Prot, 24 mg Calc. **POINTS** value: *1.*

FOOD NOTE Medium to small zucchini are more tender and flavorful than their larger counterparts. When selecting, look for zucchini that are firm and have a dark green, shiny rind. Avoid zucchini that are dull or pitted.

1 teaspoon olive oil

2 medium zucchini, thinly sliced

½ cup sliced onion

1 garlic clove, minced

¼ teaspoon salt

⅛ teaspoon crushed red pepper

4 pitted kalamata olives, chopped

2 teaspoons fresh lemon juice

2 teaspoons chopped fresh oregano

½ teaspoon grated lemon zest

Minted Zucchini and Cherry Tomato Sauté

PREP	10 MINUTES
COOK	ABOUT 5 MINUTES
SERVES	4

Heat the oil in a large nonstick skillet over medium-high heat. Add the zucchini and garlic; cook, stirring frequently, until crisp-tender, about 5 minutes. Stir in the tomatoes, salt, and pepper; cook, stirring constantly, until the tomatoes are heated through, about 1 minute. Remove the skillet from the heat; stir in the mint.

PER SERVING (about ¾ cup): 42 Cal, 2 g Fat, 0 g Sat Fat, 0 g Trans Fat, 0 mg Chol, 157 mg Sod, 7 g Carb, 2 g Fib, 2 g Prot, 21 mg Calc. **POINTS** value: *1.*

HOW WE DID IT By stirring in the mint at the end of the cooking time, we prevent it from turning an unattractive black.

1 teaspoon olive oil

3 medium zucchini, diced

1 garlic clove, minced

18 cherry tomatoes, halved

¼ teaspoon salt

⅛ teaspoon freshly ground pepper

2 tablespoons chopped fresh mint

Cajun Corn and Okra Sauté

PREP 10 MINUTES
COOK ABOUT 10 MINUTES
SERVES 6

1 Heat the oil in a large nonstick skillet over medium-high heat. Add the onion and cook, stirring occasionally, until golden, about 3 minutes.

2 Add the okra, corn, and Cajun seasoning; cook, stirring frequently, until the corn and okra are crisp-tender, about 5 minutes.

3 Remove the skillet from the heat; stir in the tomato and parsley.

PER SERVING (about ¾ cup): 91 Cal, 2 g Fat, 0 g Sat Fat, 0 g Trans Fat, 0 mg Chol, 27 mg Sod, 19 g Carb, 3 g Fib, 3 g Prot, 45 mg Calc. *POINTS* value: *1.*

GOOD IDEA For an easy main dish, stir in 1½ cups coarsely chopped ham in step 2, increase the per-serving *POINTS* value by 1, and deduct it from your **weekly POINTS Allowance.**

1 teaspoon canola oil

½ cup chopped onion

2 cups frozen cut okra, thawed

2 cups fresh or frozen corn kernels, thawed

1 teaspoon Cajun seasoning

1 medium tomato, diced

2 tablespoons chopped fresh parsley

Okra in Spiced Tomato Sauce

PREP	15 MINUTES
COOK	ABOUT 25 MINUTES
SERVES	4

1 Heat the oil in a large nonstick skillet over medium heat. Add the shallots and cook, stirring occasionally, until golden, about 4 minutes. Add the curry powder and cook, stirring constantly, until fragrant, about 30 seconds.

2 Add the tomatoes and salt; bring to a boil, breaking up the tomatoes with a wooden spoon. Add the okra; reduce the heat and simmer, covered, stirring occasionally, until the okra is tender, about 20 minutes. Stir in the parsley.

PER SERVING (¾ cup): 84 Cal, 3 g Fat, 0 g Sat Fat, 0 g Trans Fat, 0 mg Chol, 305 mg Sod, 14 g Carb, 4 g Fib, 3 g Prot, 102 mg Calc. *POINTS* value: *1.*

- 2 teaspoons olive oil
- 3 shallots, thinly sliced
- 2 teaspoons Thai red curry powder
- 1 (14½-ounce) can whole tomatoes
- ¼ teaspoon salt
- ¾ pound fresh okra, trimmed
- 1 tablespoon chopped fresh parsley

FOOD NOTE Thai red curry powder includes cayenne and chile pepper as opposed to turmeric found in regular yellow curry powder. This dish is on the spicy side, so feel free to reduce the curry powder to 1 teaspoon; it will be equally flavorful. You can also substitute regular or Madras curry powder for the red curry powder if that is more readily available.

Green Bean and Radicchio Sauté

PREP 15 MINUTES
COOK ABOUT 15 MINUTES
SERVES 4

1 Put the beans in a steamer basket; set in saucepan over 1 inch of boiling water. Cover tightly and steam the beans until crisp-tender, 7–8 minutes.

2 Meanwhile, heat the oil in a large nonstick skillet over medium-high heat. Add the onion and cook, stirring occasionally, until golden, about 5 minutes. Add the radicchio and cook, stirring frequently, until just beginning to wilt, about 1 minute. Add the garlic and cook, stirring frequently, until fragrant, about 30 seconds. Stir in the beans, salt, and pepper; cook, stirring, until the flavors are blended, about 1 minute. Remove the skillet from the heat; stir in the vinegar.

PER SERVING (1 cup): 83 Cal, 4 g Fat, 1 g Sat Fat, 0 g Trans Fat, 0 mg Chol, 304 mg Sod, 12 g Carb, 4 g Fib, 3 g Prot, 55 mg Calc. **POINTS** value: *1.*

- ¾ **pound** fresh green beans, **trimmed**
- 1 **tablespoon** extra-virgin olive oil
- 1 **onion, thinly sliced**
- 1 **small head** radicchio **(6 ounces), sliced**
- 2 garlic cloves, **minced**
- ½ **teaspoon** salt
- ⅛ **teaspoon freshly** ground pepper
- 2 **teaspoons** balsamic vinegar

TRY IT *Radicchio* (rah-DEE-kee-oh), a member of the chicory family, is renowned for the distinctive bitter accent it adds to Italian-style salads. But radicchio is also wonderful cooked, retaining its gorgeous red color in this recipe because it's only briefly sautéed.

Haricots Verts

PREP	10 MINUTES
COOK	ABOUT 5 MINUTES
SERVES	4

1 Heat the oil in a large nonstick skillet over medium-high heat. Add the garlic and cook, stirring constantly, until golden brown, 1–2 minutes.

2 Stir in the haricots verts, water, and salt; cook, covered, until the haricots verts are tender, about 2 minutes.

PER SERVING (½ cup): 48 Cal, 1 g Fat, 0 g Sat Fat, 0 g Trans Fat, 0 mg Chol, 41 mg Sod, 9 g Carb, 2 g Fib, 2 g Prot, 37 mg Calc.
POINTS value: *1.*

2 **teaspoons** olive oil

4 garlic cloves, minced

4 **cups** fresh **trimmed** haricots verts

3 **tablespoons** water

¼ **teaspoon** salt

TRY IT The slender French green beans *haricots verts* (ah-ree-koh VEHR) are a delicacy. If they are unavailable in your market, use the smallest fresh green beans you can find and increase the cooking time to about 5 minutes in step 2.

Kale with Shallots

PREP	10 MINUTES
COOK	ABOUT 30 MINUTES
SERVES	4

☑

1 Cook the kale in a large pot of boiling water until the color brightens, 15–20 seconds. Drain the kale in a colander.

2 Heat the oil in a large nonstick skillet over medium heat. Add the shallots and cook, stirring occasionally, until golden, about 3 minutes. Add the kale, broth, salt, and crushed red pepper. Cook, stirring occasionally, until the kale is tender and most of the liquid evaporates, about 15 minutes.

PER SERVING (1 cup): 80 Cal, 3 g Fat, 0 g Sat Fat, 0 g Trans Fat, 0 mg Chol, 304 mg Sod, 12 g Carb, 4 g Fib, 4 g Prot, 133 mg Calc. **POINTS** value: *1.*

GOOD IDEA If you like your greens with even more zip, substitute half the amount of kale with peppery-tasting mustard greens.

1½ **pounds kale, trimmed and coarsely chopped**

2 **teaspoons olive oil**

¼ **cup chopped shallots**

¾ **cup reduced-sodium chicken broth**

¼ **teaspoon salt**

⅛ **teaspoon crushed red pepper**

Stir-Fried Spinach

PREP	5 MINUTES
COOK	ABOUT 3 MINUTES
SERVES	4

Heat a large nonstick skillet or wok over high heat until a drop of water sizzles. Add the oil, swirl to coat the pan, then add the ginger and garlic. Stir-fry until just fragrant, about 15 seconds. Add the spinach, soy sauce, vinegar, and crushed red pepper; stir-fry until the spinach is just wilted, about 2 minutes. Serve at once.

PER SERVING (⅓ cup): 63 Cal, 2 g Fat, 0 g Sat Fat, 0 g Trans Fat, 0 mg Chol, 327 mg Sod, 9 g Carb, 6 g Fib, 7 g Prot, 224 mg Calc. **POINTS** value: *1.*

GOOD IDEA This quick and savory treatment works well on just about any leafy green; try it with mustard or turnip greens, bok choy or collards, or any other combination.

1 teaspoon canola oil

½ teaspoon minced peeled fresh ginger

1 garlic clove, minced

1 (10-ounce) bag triple-washed spinach, torn into bite-size pieces

1 tablespoon reduced-sodium soy sauce

1 tablespoon rice vinegar

Pinch crushed red pepper

Sautéed Watercress

PREP	5 MINUTES
COOK	ABOUT 5 MINUTES
SERVES	4

Heat the oil in a large nonstick skillet over medium heat. Add the garlic and cook, stirring constantly, until fragrant, about 1 minute. Add the watercress and salt; cook, stirring constantly, until just wilted, 2–3 minutes.

PER SERVING (about ½ cup): 27 Cal, 2 g Fat, 0 g Sat Fat, 0 g Trans Fat, 0 mg Chol, 160 mg Sod, 1 g Carb, 0 g Fib, 1 g Prot, 44 mg Calc. *POINTS* value: *1.*

EXPRESS LANE Since watercress grows in water, it doesn't have the grit that most greens do. Eliminating the tedious washing—just give it a quick rinse—makes this the fastest vegetable dish ever!

2 teaspoons olive oil

3 garlic cloves, minced

2 bunches watercress, cleaned

¼ teaspoon salt

Sautéed Artichoke Hearts

PREP 10 MINUTES
COOK ABOUT 15 MINUTES
SERVES 4

Heat the oil in a medium nonstick skillet over high heat. Add the artichoke hearts and cook, stirring constantly, until they just begin to brown, about 4 minutes. Stir in the tomato, basil, salt, and pepper; cook, stirring frequently, until liquid evaporates and the flavors are blended, 1–2 minutes. Spoon into the radicchio leaves.

PER SERVING (½ cup artichoke mixture with 1 radicchio leaf): 57 Cal, 2 g Fat, 0 g Sat Fat, 0 g Trans Fat, 0 mg Chol, 337 mg Sod, 8 g Carb, 4 g Fib, 2 g Prot, 31 mg Calc. **POINTS** value: **1.**

HOW WE DID IT To peel and seed a tomato, bring a small saucepan three-quarters full of water to a boil. Add the tomato and let stand 1 minute. Transfer the tomato with a slotted spoon to a cutting board. When cool enough to handle, pierce the skin of the tomato with the tip of a small knife. Loosen the skin and peel with the knife. Cut the tomato crosswise in half. Hold one tomato half in your hand over a small bowl; gently squeeze so that the seeds fall into the bowl. Repeat with the remaining tomato half; discard the skin and seeds.

2 teaspoons olive oil

1 (9-ounce) box frozen artichoke hearts, thawed

1 tomato, peeled, seeded, and diced

2 tablespoons chopped fresh basil

½ teaspoon salt

⅛ teaspoon freshly ground pepper

4 radicchio leaves

Polynesian Pineapple Chicken, page 60

Dry and Liquid Measurement Equivalents

If you are converting the recipes in this book to metric measurements, use the following chart as a guide.

TEASPOONS	TABLESPOONS	CUPS	FLUID OUNCES
3 teaspoons	1 tablespoon		½ fluid ounce
6 teaspoons	2 tablespoons	⅛ cup	1 fluid ounce
8 teaspoons	2 tablespoons plus 2 teaspoons	⅙ cup	
12 teaspoons	4 tablespoons	¼ cup	2 fluid ounces
15 teaspoons	5 tablespoons	⅓ cup minus 1 teaspoon	
16 teaspoons	5 tablespoons plus 1 teaspoon	⅓ cup	
18 teaspoons	6 tablespoons	¼ cup plus 2 tablespoons	3 fluid ounces
24 teaspoons	8 tablespoons	½ cup	4 fluid ounces
30 teaspoons	10 tablespoons	½ cup plus 2 tablespoons	5 fluid ounces
32 teaspoons	10 tablespoons plus 2 teaspoons	⅔ cup	
36 teaspoons	12 tablespoons	¾ cup	6 fluid ounces
42 teaspoons	14 tablespoons	1 cup minus 2 tablespoons	7 fluid ounces
45 teaspoons	15 tablespoons	1 cup minus 1 tablespoon	
48 teaspoons	16 tablespoons	1 cup	8 fluid ounces

VOLUME	
¼ teaspoon	1 milliliter
½ teaspoon	2 milliliters
1 teaspoon	5 milliliters
1 tablespoon	15 milliliters
2 tablespoons	30 milliliters
3 tablespoons	45 milliliters
¼ cup	60 milliliters
⅓ cup	80 milliliters
½ cup	120 milliliters
⅔ cup	160 milliliters
¾ cup	175 milliliters
1 cup	240 milliliters
1 quart	950 milliliters

LENGTH	
1 inch	25 millimeters
1 inch	2.5 centimeters

WEIGHT	
1 ounce	30 grams
¼ pound	120 grams
½ pound	240 grams
1 pound	480 grams

OVEN TEMPERATURE

250°F	120°C	400°F	200°C
275°F	140°C	425°F	220°C
300°F	150°C	450°F	230°C
325°F	160°C	475°F	250°C
350°F	180°C	500°F	260°C
375°F	190°C	525°F	270°C

NOTE: Measurement of less than ⅛ teaspoon is considered a dash or a pinch. Metric volume measurements are approximate.

Index

POINTS value Recipe Index

1 *POINTS* value

Broccoli in Oyster Sauce, 37

Cajun Corn and Okra Sauté, 228

Cumin-Scented Carrots and Sugar-Snap Peas, 183

Green Bean and Radicchio Sauté, 230

Haricots Verts, 231

Kale with Shallots, 232

Minted Zucchini and Cherry Tomato Sauté, 227

Mushroom and Cheese Omelette, 207

Okra in Spiced Tomato Sauce, 229

Sautéed Artichoke Hearts, 235

Sautéed Red Cabbage and Apples, 178

Sautéed Watercress, 234

Sautéed Zucchini with Lemon, Olives, and Oregano, 226

Stir-Fried Spinach, 233

Tuscan-Style Escarole and Cannellini Beans, 210

2 *POINTS* value

Braised Cabbage, 182

Buddha's Delight, 34

Cannellini Bean and Escarole Stew, 215

Dry-Cooked Green Beans, 185

Edamame and Shiitake Mushroom Sauté, 213

Five-Spice Tofu Stir-Fry, 131

Hot-and-Sour Cabbage, 181

Minted Succotash, 218

Sesame-Walnut Mustard Greens, 184

Spiced Barley Pilaf, 211

Warm White Bean Salad, 216

3 *POINTS* value

Beer-Braised Kielbasa with Sautéed Onions, 126

Braised Fresh Fava Beans, 176

Chicken-Spinach Stir-Fry, 63

Chickpea, Asparagus, and Corn Sauté, 212

Cornmeal-and-Almond Trout, 151

Curried Cauliflower with Black Beans, 217

Curried Turkey Stir-Fry, 119

Garlicky Seared Lamb Chops with Mint Vinaigrette, 192

Garlicky Shrimp Scampi, 156

Ginger Beef and Asparagus Stir-Fry, 10

Potato and Broccoli Rabe Skillet Pie, 222

Potato and Pepper Frittata, 133

Potato-Zucchini Pancakes, 168

Rice Pancakes with Shrimp, 128

Roast Chicken Salad, 191

Salmon Pot-Stickers with Sweet-and-Sour Dipping Sauce, 141

Sautéed Swiss Chard and Chickpeas, 173

Scrambled Tofu with Vegetables, 205

Shrimp with "Lobster" Sauce, 29

Spicy Szechuan Chicken, 16

Spicy Tangerine Beef, 110

Summer Harvest Stew, 223

4 *POINTS* value

Almond Chicken and Asparagus, 76

Asian Barley Sauté, 175

Broccoli Rabe and Rice Frittata, 134

Cajun-Style Monkfish, 150

Cellophane Noodles with Pork, 85

Chicken Chow Mein, 18

Chicken Marsala, 65

Crispy Beef with Water Chestnuts, 111

Dry-Cooked Shredded Beef, 11

Easy Skillet Chicken, 73

Fennel-Crusted Flank Steak, 189

Fragrant Rice and Black-Eyed Pea Sauté, 220

Indian Lentil and Vegetable Stew, 208

Kung Pao Chicken, 19

Lemon Capellini, 99

Lemon Chicken, 72

Lo Mein Pork and Peanut Noodles, 15

Orange Beef with Noodles, 82

Oriental Pepper Steak, 108

Piedmontese Braised Turkey, 122

Pipérade, 206

Pork and Black Bean Stir-Fry, 13

Pork and Bok Choy Stir-Fry, 113

Pork Medallions with Ginger Pears and Chutney, 45

Scallop-Cucumber Stir-Fry, 163

Seared Cod with Chunky Eggplant Sauce, 145

Shrimp Egg Fu Yung, 27

Shrimp in Lime Butter Sauce, 158

Shrimp, Pork, and Broccoli Stir-Fry, 130

Spicy Jack Cheese and Spinach Quesadillas, 51

Sweet-and-Sour Cabbage with Peanuts, 177

Tortilla Egg Roll-Ups, 48

Turkey Rolls Cordon Bleu, 47

Turkey Sausage Fajitas, 123

Vegetable and Quinoa Sauté with Orange, 137

Vegetable Lo Mein, 33

Western Omelette, 136

Zesty Chicken with Shallots, Capers, and Olives, 68

5 POINTS value

Black Bean Tostadas, 171

Buffalo Chicken Bites, 56

California Chicken Salad, 59

Caribbean Gingery Squash, Rice, and Kale, 224

Chicken and Ham "Pot Pie", 118

Cider Pork Chops, 116

Curried Fried Rice, 127

Fettuccine with Creamy Spinach Sauce, 104

Five-Treasure Rice, 24

Lemon Cod with Spinach and Potato Stew, 147

Moo Shu Turkey, 21

Pad Thai, 36

Pan-Seared Tuna Niçoise, 142

Pasta with Chickpeas, 103

Penne with Zucchini and Goat Cheese, 95

Pierogies with Creamy Mushroom and Sherry Sauce, 50

Poached Salmon with Dill-Mustard Sauce, 198

Pork with Orange-Mustard Sauce, 112

Portobello Burgers, 135

Sea Scallop Salad, 159

Shrimp Fried Rice, 25

Smoked Chicken and New Potato Hash, 195

Spaghetti with Tomatoes, Garlic, and Capers, 105

Spicy Soft-Shell Crabs, 30

Spinach Omelette, 172

Stir-Fried Noodles with Chicken, Mushrooms, and Leeks, 91

Sweet-and-Sour Turkey, 120

Tofu Teriyaki, 53

Turkey Cutlets with Cranberry-Pear Chutney, 125

Vegetable Fried Rice, 221

Warm Cassoulet Salad, 115

6 POINTS value

Chicken Calvados, 71

Chicken Ragoût with Potatoes and Olives, 79

Cider Chicken with Apples and Thyme, 69

Citrus Red Snapper, 152

Corn, Tomato, and Shrimp Sauté, 155

Crispy Cornmeal Flounder, 199

Fettuccine with Sausage and Arugula, 97

Fusilli with Swiss Chard, 102

Ginger-Pork Stir-Fry, 43

Gnocchi Marinara, 100

Hoisin Pork Stir-Fry, 41

Noodle Cake with Lamb, 88

Pan-Fried Noodles with Spicy Lamb, 86

Pineapple Pork Sauté, 44

Scallops with Salsa Cruda, 160

Sea Bass with Dill Couscous, 201

Seafood Linguine, 203

Sesame-Crusted Swordfish with Scallion Sauce, 148

Sesame-Glazed Shrimp with Snow Peas and Baby Corn, 153

Shiitake-Chicken Stir-Fry, 66

Shrimp and Scallop Paella, 202

Singapore Noodles, 22

Southwestern Skillet Macaroni and Cheese, 92

Steak with Spicy Chili Sauce, 40

7 POINTS value

Chicken Fried Rice, 77

Greek Chicken Pasta Toss, 62

Penne with Cherry Tomatoes, Provolone, and Broccoli, 98

Polenta with Vegetarian Sausage-Tomato Sauce, 204

Polynesian Pineapple Chicken, 60

Seared Scallops on Scallion Orzo, 161

Sweet-and-Sour Shrimp, 28

Veal Piccata, 46

8 POINTS value

Blackened Tuna with Rémoulade Sauce, 144

Chicken Cheddar Hoagies, 57

Paella, 164

Pan-Seared Salmon with Fresh Tomato-Basil Relish, 196

Penne with Tomato and Olive-Meat Sauce, 190

Skillet Yellow Rice and Chicken, 74

Spaghetti Bolognese, 84

Spicy Thai Beef Stir-Fry, 14

Wagon Wheels with Turkey Chili, 94

9 POINTS value

Vegetarian Fajitas, 170

Notes

Notes

Notes

Notes

Notes

Notes

Notes